A CITIZEN'S GUIDE TO PROTECTING

Wetlands & Woodlands

Neida Gonzalez

Illustrations by Jan Thornhill

FEDERATION OF
Ontario Naturalists

March 1996

Canadian Cataloguing in Publication Data

Gonzalez, Neida, 1969 –
    A citizen's guide to protecting wetlands & woodlands

Includes bibliographical references.
ISBN 1-896059-04-X

    1. Wetland conservation – Ontario – Citizen
participation. 2. Forest conservation – Ontario – Citizen
participation. 3. Nature conservation – Ontario.
4. Landscape protection – Ontario. 5. Land use –
Ontario – Planning – Citizen participation. 6. Natural
areas – Ontario. I. Thornhill, Jan   II. Federation of
Ontario Naturalists.   III. Title.   IV. Title: Wetlands &
woodlands.   V. Title: Wetlands and woodlands.

QH77.C3G65 1996   333. 7'2'09713   C96-900118-5

Production
Design and Layout Judie Shore
Printing DTP International, Toronto
Illustrations Jan Thornhill©

Contributors
Ian Attridge
Brad Cundiff
Ron Reid
Jane Roots
William B. Sargant

Published by
Federation of Ontario Naturalists
355 Lesmill Road, Don Mills, Ontario M3B 2W8
tel: (416) 444-8419, fax: (416) 444-9866
e-mail: fon@web.apc.org

© March 1996

Federation of Ontario Naturalists

The Federation of Ontario Naturalists (FON), established in 1931, is a provincially-based nongovernmental charitable organization, which protects and increases awareness of Ontario's natural areas and wildlife.

The FON currently represents 15,000 members and a network of 83 local groups—57 community based naturalists' clubs and 26 associated groups. The FON is governed by a Board of Directors that represent the individual members, naturalists' clubs and associated groups.

The FON is Ontario's leading voice in promoting the preservation of wetland habitats, the creation and management of parks, protection for Ontario's rare, threatened and endangered species and responsible forest management.

The FON publishes *Seasons*, the award-winning nature and environment magazine; produces a range of environmental education resources for schools and youth groups; and has an extensive program of trips, tours, and summer camps. As well, over the past 30 years, the FON has assembled the province's largest private nature reserve system.

Thunder Bay •

Sault Ste. Marie •

St. Joseph's Island

Federation of Ontario Naturalists
Federated Clubs and Associated Groups

Carolinian West
Essex County Field Naturalists
Sydenham Field Naturalists
Lambton Wildlife Incorporated
McIlwraith Field Naturalists of London,
  Ontario, Inc.
St. Thomas Field Naturalists Inc.
Ingersoll Nature Club
West Elgin Nature Club

Carolinian East
Woodstock Field Naturalists
Norfolk Field Naturalists
Niagara Falls Nature Club
Brant Field Naturalists
Hamilton Naturalists' Club
South Peel Naturalists' Club
Halton/North Peel Naturalists
Lower Grand River Trust Foundation
Long Point Bird Observatory
Peninsula Field Naturalists' Club
Bert Miller Nature Club of Fort Erie

Huronia
Collingwood Naturalists' Club
Brereton Field Naturalists' Club
South Lake Simcoe Naturalists' Club
Orillia Naturalists' Club
Midland-Penetang Field Naturalists
Muskoka Field Naturalists
Parry Sound Nature Club
Haliburton Highlands Field Naturalists
Huntsville Nature Club
Couchiching Conservancy
Senior League Endowment Society of
  Collingwood Inc.

Great Lakes West
Guelph Field Naturalists
Kitchener-Waterloo Field Naturalists
Upper Credit Naturalists
Saugeen Field Naturalists
Owen Sound Field Naturalists
Huron Fringe Field Naturalists
Stratford Field Naturalists

Ottawa-Frontenac
Ottawa Field Naturalists' Club
MacNamara Field Naturalists
Mississippi Valley Naturalists Club
Pembroke and Area Birding Club
Rideau Valley Field Naturalists
Upper Ottawa Valley Nature Club
Kingston Field Naturalists
Vankleek Hill Nature Society

Lake Ontario North
Brodie Club
Black Creek Conservation Project of
  Toronto Inc.
Richmond Hill Field Naturalists
West Humber Naturalists
Durham Region Field Naturalists
Pickering Naturalists
Presqu'ile-Brighton Naturalists
Willow Beach Field Naturalists
Friends of Second Marsh
Quinte Field Naturalists
Peterborough Field Naturalists Club
Kawartha Field Naturalists
Green Door Alliance
Save the Rouge Valley System
Toronto Entomologists' Association
Toronto Ornithological Club

Northern
Thunder Bay Field Naturalists
Sault Naturalists' Club of Ontario and
  Michigan
Kirkland Lake Nature Club
Temiskaming Field Naturalists
Nipissing Naturalists' Club Inc.
Sudbury Naturalists' Club
Manitoulin Nature Club

Provincially associated groups
The Canadian Wildflower Society
Fatal Light Awareness Program
Federation of Ontario Cottagers'
  Associations Inc.
Field Botanists of Ontario
Hike Ontario
Ontario Field Ornithologists
Ontario Bird Banding Association
The Quetico Foundation
Seniors for Nature
Seniors for Nature Canoe Club
Sierra Club of Eastern Canada
Wilderness Canoe Association
Wilderness Adventurers of Ontario Inc.

● **Federated Clubs**

▼ **Nature Reserves**

Kirkland Lake

Sudbury

Temiskaming

Nipissing

Upper Ottawa Valley

Pembroke

Manitoulin

MacNamara

Stewartville Swamp ▼

Ottawa

Vankleek Hill

Huntsville

Mississippi Valley

H.N. Crossley ▼

"Rubberweed" ▼

Parry Sound

Muskoka

Haliburton

Rideau Valley

Petrel Point ▼

Altberg Southern Shield ▼

Malcolm Kirk

Midland-Penetang

Couchiching

Kawartha

Owen Sound ▼

Orillia

Peterborough

Altberg Wetland

Collingwood

Brereton

South Lake Simcoe

Quinte

Kingston

Seniors League of Collingwood

Presqu'ile-Brighton

Brodie

Saugeen

Upper Credit

Richmond Hill

Durham

Willow Beach

Willoughby ▼

West Humber

Pickering ■

Second Marsh

Huron Fringe

Halton/North Peel

Credit Valley

Toronto

Guelph

South Peel

Save the Rouge Valley

George G. Newton ▼

Kitchener/Waterloo

Crozier

Green Door Alliance

Stratford

Hamilton

Black Creek

Lawson Trust Land ▼

Ingersoll

Brant

Peninsula

Niagara Falls

Wildwood

McIlwraith

Woodstock

Harold Mitchell ▼

Bert Miller

Lambton Wildlife

Norfolk

Lower Grand River

Fort Erie Conservation

Sydenham

St. Thomas

West Elgin

Long Point Bird Observatory

Essex County

▼ *Stone Road Alvar Pelee Island*

Preface

his guide has been evolving for some time, its publication continually delayed as ways to protect wetlands and woodlands changed with new legislation and programs. Significant positive developments in Ontario's land-use system have included the release of the Wetlands Policy Statement and the Natural Heritage Policy Statement, the emergence of the Conservation Land Tax Rebate Program, and amendments to the Conservation Land Act allowing conservation easements and covenants. More means to protect wetlands and woodlands are available today than ever before, but it remains up to concerned citizens to make sure these measures are implemented. The existence of legislation and policy does not guarantee that sensitive ecosystems will be protected. Naturalists everywhere must continue to work actively for habitat conservation. People like you make the difference in saving wetlands and woodlands. Today more than ever your efforts are critical.

The Federation of Ontario Naturalists (FON) is publishing this guide to provide information as well as motivation to anyone wanting to save a natural area. No matter how much time you have to contribute or whatever role you can play, large or small, your participation is essential. This guide relates experiences of people working together to protect wetland and woodland areas, profiling some "average citizens" who found they could make a difference.

This book does not provide a single recipe for successfully protecting a natural area, for every community is different, and each situation has its own complexities. Instead we provide many tools, ideas and examples of how to approach such a project.

We urge individuals and groups to begin now to work proactively towards safeguarding local natural areas. Many times, though, it will be necessary to react to sudden threats to a wetland or woodland. In most cases, a combination of approaches and ingenuity will be called for.

Your best tools will always be your instincts, tenacity and perseverance. Stick to your convictions, because the saving of any wetland or woodland is a worthwhile endeavour. Good luck in your efforts. We hope this guide makes a difference in your community's future.

Table of Contents

Introduction

atural heritage protection in Ontario has produced many success stories, about critical areas saved from development. This guide is designed to provide advice and information on how to make your own involvement in natural heritage conservation as enjoyable, efficient and effective as possible. Whether you want to protect a southern Ontario wetland threatened by bulldozers, for example, or a 150-year-old woodlot in eastern Ontario, this guide will give you some ideas on how to work towards your goal. We encourage you to take an ecosystems approach and look beyond the boundaries of the wetland or woodland. For example, a wetland is dependent on the water it receives either as discharge from a groundwater source or recharge from a watercourse. If either is cut off, the wetland may not survive.

Over the last 150 years, the landscape of Ontario has been fundamentally altered. In the regions surrounding the Great Lakes, where great expanses of pine and hardwood forests once flourished, farms, factories, shopping malls and endless rows of houses stand. In southern Ontario especially, the change has been at the expense of our wetlands and woodlands. Wetlands, regarded by many as wasted space, have been drained, filled and paved. Their immense ecological value—for flood control, in water-quality maintenance, as breeding grounds for a vast number of fish and wildlife, as storehouses of vegetative biodiversity—has been largely overlooked, as have their great social and economic values. It is estimated that south of the Canadian Shield, over 75% of all wetlands have been lost. In southwestern Ontario, the loss is nearly complete, at 90% or higher. In a world of competing land-use interests, wetlands have been consistently on the losing side.

Forest clearance is still continuing in southern Ontario, to the extent that many counties are less than 5% forested. As with wetlands, the significant ecological, social and economic roles of woodlands have been ignored. In northern Ontario, hydroelectric developments, mining operations and forestry practices are having a dramatic impact on the natural environment. Almost 90% of the logging on Crown lands is still done through clear-cutting, often devastating the natural diversity of the local forest ecosystem.

The loss of natural areas, wildlife habitat and overall biodiversity is so widespread that it has become a matter of great public concern. This public awareness is the key for any conservation effort. As the need to protect wetlands and woodlands in Ontario becomes more widely recognized there will be more opportunities to protect remaining habitat.

With continuing degradation of our vital natural systems and the slow response of political bodies, it becomes more and more evident that it is up to individuals to protect wetlands and woodlands and to stop the destruction of the landscape that supports them. It is individuals who must convince their neighbours, community leaders and government agencies to protect these areas.

Whether you want to protect a southern Ontario wetland threatened by bulldozers or a 150-year-old woodlot in eastern Ontario, this guide will give you some ideas on how to work towards your goal.

To this end, it may be necessary to band together to be most effective. Many groups are already organized and ready to take on new tasks. This guide speaks both to interested individuals and to conservation groups concerned with the protection of wetlands and woodlands.

Overview of Contents

This guide provides various tools and techniques, ideas and suggestions to help anyone interested in working towards conservation. There are various strategies to protecting wetlands and woodlands, with four areas of possible focus:

◆ changing planning through natural area studies;

◆ participating in the land-use planning process;

◆ land acquisition and stewardship; and

◆ environmental education and awareness.

No one approach alone will ensure protection of wetlands and woodlands. A coordinated effort that makes use of all opportunities is needed. However, certain individuals and groups may be better suited to working in a specific area. If you choose to do so, it is important to identify how your work can help others. For example, data from someone doing a bird inventory may be vital information for someone else trying to safeguard the area via the land-use planning process. Working together and sharing information is critical.

The areas of focus mentioned above form individual chapters of the guide, as follows:

◆ Chapter One outlines opportunities for involvement in natural area inventorying, monitoring and research. It describes the work of some naturalist groups that have achieved success in this area

◆ Chapter Two outlines the land-use planning system and the role of environmental advocacy.

◆ Chapter Three looks at land acquisition and stewardship as conservation techniques for protecting wetlands and woodlands under private ownership.

◆ The conclusion of the guide focuses on the importance of environmental education and awareness in all conservation strategies.

Deciding to affect the long-term management of a natural area is a big step for any individual or organization, whether it's in response to a crisis situation or simply out of a desire to become more actively involved. Hopefully, this guide will help answer some of the questions you have or may be facing from other members of your organization, municipal councillors or the landowners you are working with. We also hope you will share your experiences with FON staff. Conservation of natural heritage in Ontario is a dynamic and complex activity. We all have much to learn from each other. By sharing ideas and advocating for change, we will be able to make a lasting difference in the protection of Ontario's natural landscapes.

Companion Guides

FON's *Creative Conservation: A Handbook for Ontario Land Trusts*, by Stewart Hilts and Ron Reid, provides detailed information on how to establish and manage your own conservation organization or "land trust." Information on organizational issues include how to legally incorporate your group, registering as a charity, budgeting, financial management, raising funds and building memberships. *Creative Conservation* also provides detailed information on land acquisition and stewardship techniques.

The FON is publishing aids to other conservation issues in Ontario.

The Citizen's Guide to Forest Management in Ontario, going to press later this year, will outline what you can do to ensure that our northern forests are sustainably managed. Significant changes have occurred due to new legislation, notably the Crown Forest Sustainability Act, as well as the implementation of terms and conditions of the Class Environmental Assessment on Timber Management. This guide will introduce the new forestry system and how it relates to land-use planning in northern Ontario.

The *Citizen's Guide to Protecting Natural Areas through Ontario's Parks*, also to be published this year, will explain what protection Ontario parks afford natural areas through classification, zoning and management. The guide will also explain how citizens can participate in park planning and management in order to maintain and enhance the protection of natural areas within parks.

Publications may be purchased from the FON, 355 Lesmill Road, Don Mills, Ontario, M3B 2W8, (416) 444-8419.

CHAPTER ONE

Changing Planning Through
Natural Area Studies

any people believe that to save a natural area, they need to jump right in and start lobbying or implementing land-stewardship techniques. This is quite true when a site is facing an immediate threat and time does not permit for any other approaches. However, to achieve success over the long term, your efforts must be solidly based in the natural sciences. Natural area inventorying, monitoring and research are often precursors to advocacy and stewardship activities, and are always important components of any long-term strategy. Nature clubs have many amateur or professional naturalists in their membership who together have vast amounts of relevant knowledge. They should never underestimate their possible contribution to the long-term protection of wetlands and woodlands. Without the work of naturalists, many significant sites would be destroyed.

Without the work of naturalists, many significant sites would be destroyed.

Natural area inventories and research

Many times biological information on significant natural areas in a region already exists. However, the data is often scattered about in government and nongovernment offices and may not be up-to-date. A combination of research on existing biophysical information and inventories of natural areas will provide a useful tool for the protection of wetlands and woodlands. Research in this case is defined broadly to include all information gathering, analysis and synthesis. With the data obtained, your group can knowledgeably assess what wetlands and woodlands are a priority for protection. This information can then be shared with municipal staff for better planning and can be used to strengthen your arguments for protection of critical areas. In most cases municipalities' ecological information is not up-to-date, and naturalist clubs can play a significant role in filling the gaps.

Information collection is significant at every level. There is an array of possibilities for anyone interested in natural area inventories and research. On a small scale, a bird checklist could be developed for an individual wetland or woodlot. Or a group could undertake to do a biological inventory of a few selected sites. A more ambitious project would be to document significant natural areas of an entire region. All information is useful.

Various FON clubs have undertaken such inventory and research projects. Their far-ranging activities provide fine examples of what can be done. Presented below are summaries of what four groups have accomplished, as well as a case study of the extensive natural-area-inventory work done by the Hamilton Naturalists' Club.

Norfolk Field Naturalists

In 1987, the Norfolk Field Naturalists released the *Natural Areas Inventory of the Regional Municipality of Haldimand-Norfolk*. This high-quality report filled an information gap on the significant natural areas in the region. Extensive field surveys had been conducted by club staff and volunteers in 1985-86, on local amphibians, reptiles, birds, mammals, vascular plants and plant communities. Collected data was stored on a computer and analyzed. If an area met two or more predetermined criteria, the site was deemed significant.

The inventory work done by the Norfolk Field Naturalists was exceptional. With persistence and enthusiasm they were able to organize and conduct the field inventories, coordinate funding and produce a two-volume document of their results. The publication not only detailed flora, fauna, landforms and land uses of the area, but also gave credible recommendations for the protection of natural areas.

The long-term value of this study is now being recognized. In September 1995, the Regional Council of Haldimand-Norfolk adopted an official plan that protects the sites selected as environmentally significant by the Norfolk Field Naturalists. The region also incorporated the club's criteria for site selection. The official plan is now being reviewed by the Ministry of Municipal Affairs and Housing (MMAH) and should hopefully be given final approval shortly.

Lambton Wildlife Incorporated

The Lambton Wildlife Club has been busy helping to fund the acquisition of two properties located in an Area of Natural and Scientific Interest (ANSI) near Pinery Provincial Park, as well as preparing a management plan for one of them. The club also assisted the St.Clair Region Conservation Authority in purchasing the Wawanosh Wetlands in Sarnia, and a representative serves on the technical advisory committee for its management. In addition, the Lambton Wildlife group upgraded the management plans of two other properties the club owns. One is a woodlot near Sarnia, the other an oak savannah, habitat of the endangered Karner blue butterfly, as well as several other butterfly species.

KARNER BLUE / BEN AND BRENDA KOLON

In preparing the critical management plans, detailed inventory work was undertaken, as well as the compilation of existing biophysical data. Extensive information was collected on the vascular plants, vegetative communities, fungi, butterflies, birds, mammals, amphibians and reptiles found on the sites. Numerous members were involved helping to purchase the areas, collect data, develop the management plans and monitor the sites. The Lambton Wildlife group has provided another example of how inventories, research and monitoring can be used for the benefit of natural area protection.

Kitchener-Waterloo Field Naturalists

Until recently, bird records for the Regional Municipality of Waterloo had never been collected in a usable format. The Kitchener-Waterloo Field Naturalists are changing that fact, pulling together data on bird sightings collected by volunteers over the last 60 years. The information being compiled from club records, the *Atlas of Breeding Birds of Ontario*, historical sources and Ontario's Nest Record Scheme, will be stored in a database.

The new information source will be a tool for planners in the region to protect significant habitats and for the Ministry of Natural Resources (MNR) staff to monitor provincially, regionally and locally significant birds. Academic researchers will have a pool of information on breeding ranges and densities, migratory stopovers, corridors and population trends. The club will be able to monitor the status of bird populations and to update checklists for recreational and educational purposes.

The Kitchener-Waterloo club has had financial and administrative assistance from the staff of the University of Waterloo, who also helped them obtain provincial and federal grants for the project.

South Lake Simcoe Field Naturalists

Since 1985, the South Lake Simcoe Naturalists have been involved in research on wildlife and landscape ecology, as well as research into how humans perceive the environment. The core of their work has been field inventory studies. For some projects researchers have been hired on a seasonal basis, their salaries paid for through private donations and grants. Ontario's Environmental Youth Corps (EYC) program and the federal program SEED provided much-needed support.

Data accumulated for the South Lake Simcoe watershed area has been organized in a comprehensive zoological-record database, which has become a vital tool for many groups. It has been used in the master planning for York Region and most recently utilized by the Town of Georgina to prepare a natural areas study. Others who have used the database include consultants, the Interim Waste Authority, Ontario Hydro and the Ministry of Transportation.

The zoological information has been used to identify sensitive sites and indicate where development may be inappropriate.

SPRING PEEPER/ROBERT McCAW

Hamilton Naturalists' Club Natural Areas Inventory Project

 ver a period of about three years, the Hamilton Naturalists' Club completed a highly successful inventory project for the Region of Hamilton-Wentworth. In 1989, the club's conservation committee decided to explore the possibility of undertaking a field investigation of all significant natural areas in the region. To establish a baseline of information, a student was hired under a federal program (Section 25 grant) to produce an annotated bibliography of all existing data sources on environmentally significant areas. Another student was hired under a provincial program (EYC) to begin a botanical survey of the Dundas Valley.

In April 1990, club members met with staff from the Hamilton-Wentworth regional planning office, the four local conservation authorities (CAs), Ministry of Environment and

In January 1995, the Regional Municipality of Hamilton-Wentworth accepted in their official plan all of the sites that the club had identified as environmentally significant.

MNR to discuss a large-scale natural areas inventory. They were quickly informed that they had missed the deadline for funding through the budget planning process. Still, the MNR was able to find some funds to hire a biologist to survey breeding birds in the 1990 field season. Again taking advantage of the EYC program to hire a student, the club managed to have the previous season's botanical survey finished. It became apparent that government agencies could help out without supplying actual money. Both the MNR regional office and the Hamilton Region Conservation Authority freely supplied much needed office space and technical expertise.

In late summer of 1990, club members presented the government agencies with a detailed proposal for the inventory project. The comprehensive inventory was designed to be completed in one field season in order to provide timely information for the designation of new Environmentally Sensitive Areas (ESAs) in the official plan.

In the proposal, the rationale for the project was clearly explained and potential benefits described. An outline of the methodology, the responsibilities of the naturalist club as project manager and the roles of various agencies as funders and advisors was also included. A work schedule with personnel requirements was provided, with a detailed budget outlining expected sources of funding. Through club members' hard work, creativity and diligence, funding began to trickle in from foundations, government agencies and private individuals.

A project coordinator was hired in January 1991. Her role was to determine study sites, design a detailed study methodology and supervise the day-to-day operations of the project. With 85 sites identified, 15 staff were hired to survey for breeding birds, reptiles and amphibians, fish, plants, mammals and butterflies, and to enter the data into a computer. Vegetation communities were mapped for each site, with potential connecting corridors noted. The project's technical steering committee met regularly, as did the management team of club volunteers, keeping the project on course. Part of the report was published in 1993 and the remainder in 1995.

The project was a great learning opportunity for naturalists' club volunteers, leaving everyone involved very tired but with an immense sense of accomplishment and empowerment. Their work has not gone unnoticed. In January 1995, the Regional Municipality of Hamilton-Wentworth accepted in their official plan all of the sites that the club had identified as environmentally significant, with a few minor exceptions.

The club is continuing to work with the region on a greenlands strategy to link some of the sites together.

For more information, contact the Hamilton Naturalists' Club, P.O. Box 89052, Westdale Postal Outlet, Hamilton, Ontario, L8S 4R5.

Once you have identified the general area of interest, there is a lot of work to be done before beginning the inventory.

Starting your own inventory project

Clearly, not all groups can take on such an ambitious project as the Hamilton club did, but you may consider starting a smaller project. If your group is thinking about beginning an inventory of a wetland or woodland, there are many things to consider and a lot of work to be done first. Existing biophysical information needs to be gathered to ensure that you are not duplicating work, but enhancing the information base. Also, the current status of the natural area at both the municipal and regional levels needs to be ascertained to determine an appropriate strategy for protection. Information and resource needs include:

1. A detailed description of the area, including general information on species variety (both flora and fauna), the soils and drainage of the site, the general level of disturbance, surrounding land uses and how they affect the site (such as upstream erosion causing siltation in a pond).

2. Accurate maps of the natural area, on a variety of scales: air photographs, topographic maps, satellite imagery and lot and concession maps. In some areas, agencies have computerized maps on Geographic Information Systems (GIS) that can overlay different kinds of map information. GIS maps are a useful source of information and may be used to calculate information such as the percentage of forest interior or the overall canopy cover for an area. Two copies of each map will be helpful, one working copy and one spare. (For ordering maps, see Information Sources at the end of this chapter.)

3. Existing wetland and woodland inventory work from the local CA and the MNR. This data may be dated or done on a regional scale, but valuable insights may be gleaned from it. CA and MNR staff may be good sources of information, as they often have personal experience in an area you may be interested in.

4. Any additional ecological information. Other sources include naturalist clubs, individual naturalists, community land-use planning committees, local environmental consultants, colleges and universities, as well as the science departments of local high schools.

5. Information on any special or recognized ecological status of the wetland or woodland areas. Have any sites been identified as an ANSI by the MNR or an ESA by the municipality? Have any species-at-risk been documented in the area?

6. Whether any government agency or conservation group has an interest in the protection of the area.

7. Municipal zoning for the wetland and woodland areas. Additionally, determine if there are any references about wetlands or woodlands in the official plan.

When all this information has been collected, your group should have:

◆ a foundation of ecological, geographical and political information;

◆ maps and air photos for discussion and presentation use;

◆ an idea of what your objectives might be for the area (a vision of what you would like to see);

◆ "area of interest" lines drawn on the maps, indicating the size of the project and location of the most sensitive core areas.

With this knowledge base, gaps in information that your group can fill through inventories can be established. Government agencies and other conservation groups may be able to help with funds, technical expertise and administrative services. A proposal outlining the scope of the study, methods, budget and timeline can then be produced. Remember to get landowner permission before entering a property to gather information. If approached in the right way, landowners are often quite willing to allow access to their land for research purposes.

Keeping in mind an ecosystem approach, some questions an inventory might be able to address include:

◆ How big a protected area is required to maintain the integrity and character of the wetland or woodland?

◆ Are some features more vulnerable or threatened than others? Where are they in relation to one another and the developed areas?

◆ Where are the important sites for significant species?

◆ How large a buffer is reasonably required to protect the wetland or woodland from encroachment or conflicting land use?

◆ Will it be possible to protect the features you are interested in without constant management or intervention?

SANDY SYMMES

Participating in established wildlife and natural area monitoring projects

Interested individuals may be able to take part in existing monitoring projects. Wildlife and natural area studies have many uses. They can update natural area inventories and provide needed information to national and provincial studies of wildlife trends, so that significant population declines can be identified. Monitoring can also provide information on site-specific wildlife trends. Currently, a new community-based approach to monitoring is being looked at by the Canadian Wildlife Service (CWS). There are many new wildlife survey projects being planned.

To find out if any monitoring projects are taking place in your community, call CWS, the Long Point Bird Observatory (LPBO), or the Natural Heritage Information Centre (NHIC). You can also contact conservation groups, the MNR and CAs. The table below outlines some of the programs available. (Names and list of contacts are provided at the end of the chapter under Information Sources.)

Table 1: Monitoring Projects

PROGRAM NAME	TIME COMMITMENT	SKILLS REQUIRED	LOCATION AND CONTACT
Christmas Bird Count	one day per year near Christmas	beginners to experienced birders	about 80 cities and towns in Ontario; contact your local naturalist club
Project Feeder Watch	observe twice every two weeks November to March	ability to recognize about 25 common feeder birds	anywhere in Ontario; contact LPBO
Canadian Lakes Loon Survey	check lake(s) once during each of June, July and August	identify common loon; good observational skills	anywhere in Ontario; contact LPBO
Amphibians: Backyard Surveys	three minutes every evening from April to August	ability to identify ten frog songs	your own backyard; contact CWS
Amphibians: Road Call Counts	three evenings each spring from March to July	ability to identify ten frog songs	seven-km routes on back roads by car; contact CWS
Ontario Nest Records Scheme	one or more visits to an active nest or nests	ability to identify any bird's active nest	anywhere in Ontario; contact the Royal Ontario Museum
Marsh Monitoring Program	two or three evenings each spring from April to July	ability to identify frog calls and/or marsh birds	throughout Ontario; contact LPBO
Ontario Birds at Risk	variable, depending on activity	beginners to experienced birders	throughout Ontario; contact LPBO
Hawk Watching	one or more days in spring and fall	ability to identify raptors; all welcome to assist	several stations in Ontario; (see Information Sources)

PROGRAM NAME	TIME COMMITMENT	SKILLS REQUIRED	LOCATION AND CONTACT
Migration Monitoring	days to weeks (longer-term volunteer preferred)	all levels; beginners can be trained	Long Point, Thunder Cape; contact LPBO
Monitoring Avian Productivity	nine six-hour sessions from June through August	experienced birders and banders	several stations in Ontario; contact CWS
Forest Bird Monitoring Program	two mornings in late May or June, each year	ability to identify forest birds by song and sight	throughout Ontario; contact CWS
Breeding Bird Survey	one morning in June, every year	ability to identify breeding birds	throughout Ontario; contact LPBO

Information sources

Maps

TOPOGRAPHIC (TOPO) MAPS:

1:10,000 and 1:20,000 black-and-white topo maps are available from the Natural Resources Information Centre (NRIC). If you do not know the number of the map you are looking for, call the NRIC collect at (416) 314-2000 and ask for an index. Each map costs about $6.25 plus tax. New colour air photos are currently being photographed for southern Ontario.

NRIC
First Floor, Macdonald Block
900 Bay St, Toronto, Ontario, M7A 2C1

1:50,000 topo maps are produced by the federal government and are available through commercial map dealers (check in the yellow pages), or from Natural Resources Canada.

Natural Resources Canada
Survey and Mapping Branch
Ottawa, Ontario, K1A 0H3

WETLAND, ANSI AND RARE SPECIES MAPPING

Mapping of these features at various scales is available from local MNR offices or from the NHIC.

NHIC
Box 7000, Peterborough,
Ontario, K9J 8M5
(705) 745-6767

FLOOD PLAIN MAPPING

Flood plain mapping is available from all conservation authorities. In most cases it is possible to obtain a copy of a flood plain map for approximately $8.00. How to reach conservation authorities is outlined below in the government agency section.

AIR PHOTOS

Air photos are available from NRIC; when ordering send the legal description of the property, including municipal jurisdiction (e.g., township and county). The cost of each standard-size, current-year air photo is $8.25 plus taxes. Nonstandard air photos can cost much more.

Catalogues are available from some local MNR offices.

TOWNSHIP PLAN MAPS

Maps that show lot and concession numbers are available from the Crown Land Registry of the MNR. They can be reached at (416) 314-1397.

Crown Land Registry
90 Sheppard Ave East
North York, Ontario, M2N 1A3

ONTARIO TRANSPORTATION MAP SERIES

There are eight Ontario region maps at a scale of 1:250,000 available from the Ministry of Transportation. Each costs $7.00 plus tax, or all eight can be purchased for $49.00 plus tax. The ministry has a toll-free number, 1-800-387-0141, or if you are in the Toronto area, phone (416) 445-3333.

Ministry of Transportation
Map Unit, East Building — Lower Level
1201 Wilson Avenue
Downsview, Ontario M3M 1J8

AGRICULTURAL CAPABILITY MAPS AND DRAINAGE MAPS

Available from the Ministry of Agriculture, Food and Rural Affairs (519) 767-3587.

Ministry of Agriculture , Food and
Rural Affairs
Resources Management Branch
P.O. Box 1030
52 Royal Road
Guelph, Ontario
N1H 1G3

SATELLITE IMAGERY

Ontario Hydro and MNR have extensive satellite imagery and land-cover mapping (GIS maps) in Ontario. A map sheet of a specific area can be printed for approximately $50.00 by Ontario Hydro. For more information contact Ms. Nargis Ladha at (416) 592-8240.

Ontario Hydro
Transmission Project Division
Geomatic Section
700 University Avenue ,
Toronto, Ontario, M5G 1X6

Provincial Remote Sensing Office
90 Sheppard Avenue East
North York, Ontario, M2N 1A3
(416) 314-1312

Government Agencies

General inquiries about any government agency or program can be made by calling:

326-1234 *local call from Toronto
675-7729 *local call from London
238-3630 *local call from Ottawa
675-4574 *local call from Sudbury
475-1110 *local call from Thunder Bay
1-800-267-8097 *toll free from 416, 905, and some areas within 705 and 519 (Barrie, Muskoka, Parry Sound, Brant and Lindsay /Peterborough)
1-800-268-8758 *toll free from 613 area code

All others in Ontario can call Bell Operator for Zenith Ontario.

ONTARIO GOVERNMENT BOOKSTORES

880 Bay Street
Toronto, Ontario, M7A 1N8

KPL Government Bookstore
200 King Street West
Kitchener, Ontario, N2G 4V6

Windsor Public Library Bookstore
850 Ouellette Avenue
Windsor, Ontario, N9A 4M9

Access Ontario
Rideau Centre Mall
Ottawa, Ontario, K1N 9J7

Renouf Publishing Company
61 Sparks Street,
Ottawa, Ontario, K1P 5A5

MUNICIPALITIES

A municipal directory can be obtained from all government bookstores.

MINISTRY OF NATURAL RESOURCES

Information on any of the MNR offices or programs is available through the Natural Resources Information Centre, (416) 314-2000.

A government telephone directory may also be helpful. These can be obtained from any government bookstore.

The MNR library may also be a useful source of information. Call ahead to make an appointment:(416) 314-1208.

Ministry of Natural Resources Library
90 Sheppard Avenue East, 5th Floor
North York, Ontario, M2N 1A3

CONSERVATION AUTHORITIES

To get a current list of conservation authorities' addresses and telephone numbers, contact the MNR at (905) 713-7728.

Conservation Authorities
Operations Unit
Ministry of Natural Resources
50 Bloomington Road West, R.R. #2
Aurora, Ontario, L4G 3G8

Monitoring Projects

Breeding Bird Survey
BBS Ontario Coordinator
LPBO,
Box 160, Port Rowan,
Ontario, N0E 1M0
(519) 586-3531
fax: (519) 586-3532

Ontario Birds at Risk
Audrey Heagy, LPBO

Marsh Monitoring Program
Amy Chabot, LPBO

Migration Monitoring Program
Jon McCracken, LPBO

Canadian Lakes Loon Survey
Harry Vogel, LPBO

Project FeederWatch
LPBO

Hawk Watching
1) Niagara Peninsula
(March 1 to May 15)
Glenn Barnett
87 Highland Park Dr.,
Dundas, Ontario, N9H 6G5

2) Hawk Cliff
(Mid-August to Dec. 30)
Marge Bowlby
29 Gustin St.,
Lambeth, Ontario, N0L 1S3

3) Cranberry Marsh
(September 1 to November 30)
John Barker
37 Elmsthorpe Ave.,
Toronto, Ontario, M5P 2L5

Forest Bird Monitoring Program
Mike Cadman
CWS
Environment Canada
75 Farquhar St., Guelph,
Ontario, N1H 3N4
(519) 826-2094
Fax: (519) 826-2113

Amphibian Surveys
Christine Bishop
CWS
867 Lakeshore Road, Box 5050
Burlington, Ontario, L7R 4A6
(905) 336-4968

Ontario Nest Records Scheme
Ross James or George Peck
Department of Ornithology
Royal Ontario Museum
100 Queen's Park,
Toronto, Ontario, M5S 2C6
(416) 586-5521
fax: (416) 586-5863

Useful documents

SAW-WHET OWL/ROBERT McCAW

Austen, M.J.W., M.D. Cadman and
R.D. James. 1994. *Ontario Birds at
Risk: Status and Conservation Needs.*
Federation of Ontario Naturalists
and Long Point Bird Observatory.
Don Mills and Port Rowan

Bishop, C.A. and K.E. Pettit (Eds.).
1992. *Declines in Canadian
Amphibian Populations: Designing a
National Monitoring Strategy*
Occasional Paper 76. Canadian
Wildlife Service, Environment
Canada. Ottawa

Cadman, M.D., P.F.J. Eagles and F.M.
Helleiner (Eds.). 1987. *Atlas of the
Breeding Birds of Ontario.* University
of Waterloo Press. Waterloo

Dobbyn, Jon (Sandy). 1994. *Atlas of
the Mammals of Ontario.* Federation
of Ontario Naturalists. Don Mills

Environment Canada. 1995. *Wildlife
Watchers: Report on Monitoring.* Issue
Number 1. Canadian Wildlife
Service. Guelph

Federation of Ontario Naturalists.
Seasons

Gartshore, M.E., D.A. Sutherland and
J.D. McCracken. 1987. *The Natural
Areas Inventory of the Regional
Municipality of Haldimand-Norfolk,*
Volumes 1 and 2. Norfolk Field
Naturalists. Simcoe

Heagy, Audrey E. (Ed.). 1993.
*Hamilton-Wentworth Natural Area
Inventory.* Volume 2. Hamilton
Naturalists' Club. Hamilton

Heagy, Audrey E. (Ed.). 1995.
*Hamilton-Wentworth Natural Area
Inventory.* Volume 1. Hamilton
Naturalists' Club. Hamilton

Hilts, S.G., M.D. Kirk, R.A. Reid and
contributors. 1986. *Islands of Green.*
Ontario Heritage Foundation.
Toronto

National Wildlife Research Centre.
1994. *Canadian Land Bird
Monitoring Strategy.* Migratory Bird
Populations Division, Canadian
Wildlife Service. Hull, Quebec

Riley, J.L. and P. Mohr. 1994. *The
Natural Heritage of Southern
Ontario's Settled Landscapes:
A Review of Conservation and
Restoration Ecology for Land-use and
Landscape Planning.* Ontario
Ministry of Natural Resources.
Aurora

CHAPTER TWO

Getting Involved
In Land-use Planning

his chapter focuses on the role you can play in the land-use planning process for the protection of wetlands and woodlands. Basic information on the planning system and possible approaches you can take when intervening will be discussed. Opportunities and obstacles will be outlined. The significant part some citizens have played in protecting wetlands and woodlands through environmental advocacy will be looked at.

Specifically, this chapter outlines:

◆ new planning tools for protecting wetlands and woodlands;
◆ how the municipal system works;
◆ issues at the municipal level;
◆ how citizens can get involved in land-use planning;
◆ steps to take when a wetland or woodland is threatened;
◆ the Niagara Escarpment as a special land-use planning area.

Revisions to the Planning Act occurred in 1995 in response to the Commission on Planning and Development Reform (Sewell Commission). In 1996, additional and more fundamental changes are being implemented—the trend being for more control at the local level and less provincial direction. Citizen participation in all communities is therefore crucial for the conservation of remaining wetlands and woodlands.

Understanding how municipalities work is important, as they have a significant role to play in habitat conservation. Local governments are responsible for deciding how and where land will be developed within their jurisdictions. Land-use planning is arguably the single most important function of a municipality. Municipal authority for planning is obtained from the province, which theoretically provides overall policies through the Planning Act. However, until the release of the Wetlands Policy Statement in 1992, no policy under the Planning Act addressed the need to protect significant habitat in Ontario. This policy vacuum has created a situation where many municipalities made decisions on an ad-hoc basis, with far too little analysis or understanding of the environmental implications. Development at the expense of wetlands and woodlands has been the norm, even in areas of the Canadian Shield, where the historic losses of wetlands and woodlands have been greater than 75%.

During these difficult times, there have always been citizens who fought for the protection of natural areas at the municipal level. Two such people, Jack and Margaret Cranmer-Byng, have dedicated much time and effort to protecting significant habitat through the land-use planning process. Their work has been exemplary.

PROFILE

Jack and Margaret Cranmer-Byng

"It's easy to say you have too much to do. You just have to go ahead and get involved anyway.

For Jack and Margaret Cranmer-Byng, getting involved in local land-use issues is a matter of protecting the place you live, whether it's Hong Kong, downtown Toronto or southern York Region.

Jack says he first became aware of the deteriorating state of the environment while teaching in Hong Kong. As avid birders, he and his colleagues realized "things were not so good — we were losing our birds and losing the places the birds inhabited." Shortly thereafter, he and Margaret immigrated to Toronto, and Jack found an interesting ravine near their new home that during spring migration was popular with many warblers.

All around, however, wild places were disappearing as development boomed throughout the 1970s. Jack quickly realized that "it wasn't enough to say 'too bad,' I had to do something." He started by conducting Toronto's first ravine survey with two other interested members of the Toronto Field Naturalists, in Chatsworth Ravine, the green space near his home he had come to know through birding.

The group's meticulously detailed findings "gave us

some leverage" and helped convince the parks department that the ravine needed better protection. Jack notes that keeping the local councillor informed and on side also gave their cause a boost.

The timing of the survey meshed nicely with the City of Toronto's first attempt to pass a ravine-protection by-law, adds Margaret, and Jack made deputations in support of the proposed law. Meanwhile, the Toronto Field Naturalists, having seen the success of the first survey, continued the work on other ravines and natural areas in the city.

Jack used his own experiences and those of others to co-produce a book, *Urban Natural Areas: Ecology and Preservation,* but he says the biggest lesson he learned is that "it's easy to say you have too much to do. You just have to go ahead [and get involved] anyway. The great thing is it's a learning process for you while you're doing it."

Margaret, for one, took Jack's advice to heart and in the 1980s got involved in a local issue near where they were then living in Thornhill: a developer planned to build housing on a golf course that included high-quality wooded areas. "Jack's contacts with the field naturalists were very useful. We got people out to do a thorough inventory and then went to council," she explains. The council turned the developer down, but he appealed to the Ontario Municipal Board (OMB).

The Uplands Golf Course in Thornhill includes high-quality wooded areas.

25

JACK AND MARGARET CRANMER-BYNG

Tributary of the Don River on the Uplands Golf Course

The ratepayer group to which Margaret belonged countered by hiring a lawyer and raising funds. The result was a compromise agreement under which the City of Vaughan used $6 million from its park fund to buy a significant piece of the golf-course tablelands.

"We didn't get everything we wanted," Margaret notes, but the gains were enough to keep her interested in the city's official-plan process, which was just getting underway. Five years later, she's looking forward to the conclusion of that undertaking and is also deeply involved in efforts to protect the Oak Ridges Moraine as a whole.

Margaret feels that bureaucrats and politicians are more willing to listen to citizens with environmental concerns these days. "The governments and ministries and conservation authorities are all putting on a much more green image. They may not always follow through," she adds, "but it helps."

A good example is the Metro Toronto Region Conservation Authority, Jack says. When he was active in the '70s, "we hated them, and our feelings were justified. But they have changed tremendously."

But even if agencies and governments are putting on a friendlier face, the rule is still "be prepared," Margaret cautions. If a woodlot in your community is threatened, you have to find out what is in that forest. Join the local naturalist club and get members involved in studying the area, she suggests, and then talk to the local planner and find out what tools, such as zoning by-laws, might be available.

"You have to presume that people are willing to listen and are interested, and you have to ask for their help," she concludes. "Only when you are sure they are not going to help do you make things difficult for them."

Nothing in the new policies prevents planning authorities from going beyond the minimum standards established.

New tools: policy statements

New tools that Jack and Margaret Cranmer-Byng did not have at their disposal in the '70s and '80s are now available for protecting habitat. Today there are policy statements under the Planning Act that government agencies must address. The protection of natural-heritage values was first dealt with in this way in 1995, when the Comprehensive Set of Policy Statements was released. The natural heritage section of this document incorporated the 1992 Wetlands Policy Statement and began to address many concerns about the protection of natural ecosystems. In 1996, the Policy Statements were revised by the new government. As policy statements are not legislation per se, they can be easily amended by the government of the day. The consequence of the 1996 revisions has been an overall reduction in environmental protection. However, the new policies are still a strong tool that can be used in defense of natural ecosystems.

Nothing in the new policies prevents planning authorities from going beyond the minimum standards established. There is no reason that municipalities should not be encouraged to use the 1995 Comprehensive Set of Policy Statements when planning for development. A review of the natural heritage sections of both documents is on page 28.

The scope for environmental protection through the Planning Act in Ontario has been limited by the new policies. Development is no longer restricted within many natural features such as: sensitive groundwater recharge areas, headwater and aquifer areas, significant ravines, river and stream corridors, significant shorelines of lakes, rivers and streams, habitat of vulnerable species, and significant natural corridors. Also, there has been a considerable reduction in protection for wetlands. By changing the boundary from the Great Lakes/St. Lawrence Region to south and east of the Canadian Shield the area where the Wetlands Policy applies has been cut by 50%. However, there is enough substance in the 1996 Proposed Policy Statement to pursue the protection of natural areas with municipalities.

WOODLAND TRAIL/JACK AND MARGARET CRANMER-BYNG

Comprehensive Set of Policy Statements, 1995

There are two goals stated with respect to natural heritage in the 1995 policies:

1) To protect the quality and integrity of ecosystems, including air, water, land, and biota; and, where quality and integrity have been diminished, to encourage restoration or remediation to healthy conditions.

POLICIES UNDER GOAL ONE

◆ Development may be permitted only if the quantity and quality of ground water and surface water are protected. Development that will negatively impact on areas identified as sensitive ground water recharge areas, headwaters and aquifers will not be permitted.

◆ Development will not be permitted in significant ravine, valley, river and stream corridors, and in significant portions of the habitat of endangered species and threatened species.

◆ No development is permitted, or development may be permitted only if it does not negatively impact the natural features or the ecological functions for which the area is identified in respect to the habitat of vulnerable species, significant natural corridors, significant woodlands south and east of the Canadian shield, areas of natural and scientific interest, shorelines of lakes, rivers and streams, and significant wildlife habitat.

◆ Development will not be permitted on adjacent lands if it negatively impacts the natural features or the ecological functions for which the area is identified.

◆ Development may be permitted if it does not harmfully alter, disrupt or destroy fish habitat.

◆ In decisions regarding development, every reasonable opportunity should be taken to: maintain the quality of air, land and water, and biota; maintain biodiversity compatible with indigenous natural systems; and protect natural links and corridors; the improvement and enhancement of these features and systems is encouraged.

POLICIES UNDER GOAL TWO

◆ No development is allowed within provincially significant wetlands (Class 1, 2 and 3) in the Great Lakes — St. Lawrence Region (area south of Sault Ste. Marie and Temagami).

◆ In the Great Lakes — St. Lawrence Region on adjacent lands, development may be permitted only on the main conditions that development does not result in loss of wetland functions or loss of contiguous wetland areas. This shall be demonstrated by an environmental impact study (EIS).

◆ In the Boreal Region, development is allowed on the main condition that there is no loss of wetland function. This shall be demonstrated by an EIS.

◆ Municipalities are encouraged to protect wetlands that are not provincially significant (Classes 4 — 7).

◆ New utilities/facilities shall be located outside provincially significant wetlands wherever possible.

Proposed Policy Statement, 1996

POLICIES

Natural heritage features and areas will be protected from incompatible development.

◆ Development and site alteration will not be permitted in significant portions of the habitat of endangered and threatened species, and in significant wetlands south and east of the Canadian Shield.

◆ Development and site alteration may be permitted in fish habitat, in signifi-

cant wetlands on the Canadian Shield, in significant woodlands south and east of the Canadian Shield, in significant valleylands south and east of the Canadian Shield, in significant wildlife habitat, and in significant areas of natural and scientific interest, if it has been demonstrated that it will not negatively impact the natural features or the ecological functions for which the area is identified.

◆ Development and site alteration may be permitted on adjacent lands if it has been demonstrated that it will not neg-

atively impact the natural features of the ecological functions for which the area is identified. The diversity of natural features in an area and the natural connections between them should be maintained, and improved where possible.

◆ The quality and quantity of ground water and surface water and the function of sensitive ground water recharge/discharge areas, aquifers and headwaters will be maintained or enhanced.

Protection of wetlands and woodlands is not guaranteed by the mere existence of policy statements. They have to be implemented by all municipalities in Ontario.

Implementation Guidelines

The Implementation Guidelines are another useful tool. These guidelines are intended to help the public and those implementing the policies to interpret and adequately address what standards should be used to categorize specific natural features as significant. Municipalities are allowed to develop comparable standards. Compare the standards in the implementation guidelines with those of your municipality.

The new edition of the implementation guidelines expected in the spring of 1996 should include a description of performance indicators that will be used to monitor how the natural heritage policies have been executed. These performance indicators may be a good tool to determine whether municipalities have identified, and evaluated the natural heritage features and areas specified in the policy. Included in this may be how municipalities assess the possible negative impacts of development.

In implementing the policy statements some municipalities will be able to refer to watershed, subwatershed plans or master drainage plans, as well as targets set by CAs, MNR and Ministry of Environment and Energy (MOEE) for water quantity and quality. Find out what resources your municipality has at its disposal (see Useful Documents at the end of this chapter).

Protection of wetlands and woodlands is not guaranteed by the mere existence of policy statements. They have to be implemented by all municipalities in Ontario. How can the public ensure that these policies are complied with and implemented at the municipal level?

What opportunities exist for citizens to ensure the implementation of the policy statements? These questions will be answered in the section Getting Involved.

MARK STABB

Before you can participate in the land-use planning process you should know some basic facts about your municipality and how the whole system works.

Before you can participate in the land-use planning process you should know some basic facts about your municipality and how the whole system works. Municipalities are not all the same. Each has varying resources, capabilities and willingness to implement provincial policies. The following section, Knowing Your Municipality, will delineate the different types of local governments which are responsible for land-use planning, and what issues you may face at the municipal level.

Knowing your municipality

There are 816 municipalities listed in the 1995 Ontario municipal directory, approximately 80% of them in southern Ontario. Many parts of the northern area of the province are not municipally organized, or else have a single-tier municipal structure. Due to the significant difference in the planning systems and conservation issues there, the publication *Citizen's Guide to Forest Management in Ontario* will outline the land use-planning process in the north.

In southern Ontario, land-use planning occurs within two different municipal structures, each being a two-tiered system. The first is county government, where the upper tier is the county and the lower tier is either the township, town or village. The majority of municipalities use this system. The second option is regional government, consisting of an upper-tier regional municipality and lower-tier townships, villages, towns and cities.

Upper-tier municipalities

In the 1995 Planning Act revisions, the province gave all regional municipal governments approval authority over lower-tier municipal official plans and plan amendments. The 1996 amendments extend approval authority to all counties once their updated official plans come into effect. The province has devolved a great portion of its approval authority to the upper-tier municipalities, giving county and regional governments a prominent role in directing land-use planning in Ontario.

Regional municipal governments, formed in the '60s and early '70s, exercise more powers than do counties and generally have all or partial responsibility for water supply and sewage disposal. The 13 regional governments in southern Ontario contain the majority of the province's population. The traditional roles of upper-tier municipalities are to provide services that cannot be effectively handled by local municipalities.

In both county and regional structures, the upper-tier governments do not collect taxes, but exact funds from lower-tier municipalities. In addition, upper-tier councils are not elected directly, but are made up of councillors elected at the lower tiers.

In the county system most of the land area is usually rural. Among lower-tier municipalities, townships are considered a rural unit, while villages and towns are considered small urban pockets.

Lower-tier municipalities

The majority of local land-use decisions are made by lower-tier municipalities via their official plans. Lower-tier municipal plans are required to be in conformity with those of the upper tier. However, if proposed amendments to the Planning Act are adopted, the Minister of Municipal Affairs and Housing will be able to exempt municipalities from having their official plans and official-plan amendments approved by the upper-tier government.

At the lower tier, councillors are elected every three years. The majority of land-use decisions are made by the municipal council. As stated earlier, lower-tier municipalities collect property taxes for both themselves and the upper tier. In general, urban municipalities have greater financial resources than rural ones. This in part explains significant differences in the number and level of services offered by urban and rural municipalities. Often the ability of municipalities to plan adequately for the protection of natural areas will depend on their financial resources. In many cases, school boards and the county or regional government claim more than 75% of revenues collected.

Issues at the municipal level

Certain issues will emerge when you are dealing with wetland and woodland protection through the land-use planning process, including:

♦ Inadequate funding and not enough staff;
♦ Local autonomy from the province;
♦ Private property rights

To provide a general idea of what problems might be encountered at the municipal level, these issues will be discussed briefly. Depending on the municipality, some may not be relevant, but you should be aware of them as possible concerns in your pursuit of wetland/woodland conservation.

Inadequate funding and not enough staff

As already documented, the majority of municipalities do not have adequate funding or staff to administer additional programs, especially in rural areas. Implementation of the policy statements under the Planning Act does require a long-term financial commitment, and with provincial government cutbacks some municipalities may not be able to meet present responsibilities, let alone take on additional work.

If your municipality is not implementing the policy statements, find out if it is because of financial difficulties or staff shortages. It may be up to citizens' groups to help municipalities meet their responsibilities, by taking on tasks such as identifying environmentally sensitive areas. In addition, it may be up to citizens' groups to help municipalities lobby for adequate funding.

As citizens of Ontario you have the right to expect that provincial policy be adhered to at the municipal level.

Local autonomy from the province

In drafting or revising official plans, or in day-to-day land-use planning, some municipalities may not be interested in adhering to provincial policy. They may have a negative view towards the provincial level of government. There is a misconception on the part of a few municipalities that their right to local autonomy is being suppressed, when in fact the province has always had the constitutional right to execute land-use planning in Ontario. Municipalities are creations of the province and have been given discretionary powers to conduct land-use planning under the province's direction.

Complying with provincial policy should not be a matter of municipal choice. As citizens of Ontario you have the right to expect that provincial policy be adhered to at the municipal level.

Private-property rights

Many people endorse the need for good planning as long as the measures do not affect how they may develop their own property. In some cases, when it is suggested that a wetland or woodland be put in a "zone with restricted or no development," property owners may protest that it amounts to expropriation without compensation. That claim is unfounded, as it is the government's prerogative to put the rights of the community before the rights of an individual.

Property rights in Canada, set out in what is called the common law, have never been absolute. Property rights are also set out in planning law, so that property owners can do with their property whatever the law says and no more. It is law in Canada that "compensation does not follow zoning either up or down." In other words, if the zoning on your property is changed so that its value increases, you are not required to compensate the government. It also means that if your property value decreases because of a change in zoning, the government is not required to compensate you.

For well-planned communities, where orderly growth minimizes servicing costs and environmental integrity is adequately protected, it may be necessary to restrict the development rights of the individual for the greater good of the greater number.

However, in spite of the appropriateness of restrictive zoning in certain situations, the attitude that private-property rights are the same as development rights, and are inviolate remains. Be prepared to deal with this issue. It may come up in discussions at either municipal level.

Getting involved

Municipalities use three main tools for planning: official plans, zoning by-laws and land severances/subdivisions. As well, advisory committees to municipal councils are sometimes used in planning matters. Opportunities available for citizen participation through each planning tool will be examined below.

Official plans

Most municipalities of both tiers develop official plans to outline their policies dealing with matters such as land severance, plans of subdivision and the protection of natural areas. The plans describe land-use designations, indicating what type of development, if any, is allowed within specific areas. Overall, the plan should indicate the type and rate of future physical growth in a municipality. As mentioned above, lower-tier official plans should comply with that of the upper tier.

An official plan is the only tool that looks at planning in the long term at the municipal level. However, such a plan does not outline how a landowner may or may not develop his/her property. This is done through a zoning by-law.

Provincial policy statements should be incorporated into every new official plan. Contact your municipal clerk and find out when the official plan in your municipality will next be reviewed. If your municipality does not have an official plan, ask when they will develop one.

Within the plan-development process there is a requirement for extensive public consultation before approval of an official plan is granted. This is your chance to speak out and have local wetlands and woodlands designated for protection. If you have participated in the development of an official plan and are still not satisfied with the outcome, you can appeal the plan's approval to the OMB. Plan approval is generally given by MMAH or the upper-tier municipality; however, proposed amendments to the Planning Act may result in lower-tier municipalities approving their own official plans. Also, keep in mind that amendments to the Planning Act are expected to reduce the time period in which you can file for an appeal, from 30 days to 20 from the date of official-plan approval.

If an approved official plan is in place, each local council must hold a public meeting at least once every five years to review the plan and consider whether it needs to be updated or changed. That's the time to make sure the areas you are concerned with are protected.

There may not be a review coming up and you might think that waiting two or three years to implement the policy statements is too long. You have the option of requesting an amendment to the official plan to have conservation issues addressed. Your municipal clerk or planner should be able to provide you with the application requirements. Be persistent; sometimes it takes a long time to get an issue addressed. Unfortunately, current changes to the Planning Act will enable councils to waive the requirement for a public meeting when an amendment to the official plan is requested if the council considers the amendment request inappropriate.

Other groups such as developers may present official-plan amendments. If you have concerns with proposed amendments, send your written comments to the municipality or go to the public meeting. You can also appeal amendments to the OMB.

WARNING...

The Planning Act now stipulates that, to have the right to appeal a decision to the OMB, you must make written or oral comments to council on draft official plans or plan amendments before they are approved. Pay close attention to the decisions your council is making.

33

Zoning by-laws

Zoning by-laws have two main components:

1) the designation of various areas of land (or zones) within which specified categories of land use are permitted or prohibited; and
2) regulations explaining the conditions under which land may be used within each zone.

Zoning by-laws have to conform with the official plan of the municipality. It is within zoning by-laws that protection of actual wetland and woodland sites can occur. As with official plans, public consultation is required for zoning by-law creation or amendment. This is a good opportunity to designate wetlands and woodlands for protection. Municipalities are obligated to give notice of public meetings, usually through local newspapers. It is critical to have wetlands and woodlands designated for protection both in the official plan and in the zoning by-laws.

Zoning by-law decisions by municipal councils can be appealed to the OMB. Again, warning issued for appeals to the OMB applies to zoning by-laws: to have the right to appeal you must have participated in the municipal consultation process.

Land severances and subdivisions

A land severance is the approved splitting of one parcel of land into two separate properties, while a plan of subdivision is used to divide land into more than two or three parcels. Properties are usually divided so the owner can give, sell or lease one or more parcels. Inappropriate development through plans of subdivision and random severancing poses a major threat to wetlands and woodlands. Fragmentation of natural areas frequently results from land division. In addition, a proliferation of new lots that are too small or otherwise ill suited for the proper functioning of septic systems has contributed to water degradation. However, there are opportunities for citizens to participate and influence the land-division process.

For land severances, more commonly called consents, there is a limited opportunity to participate. The requirement for a public meeting has been eliminated in new changes to the Planning Act. Usually, the lower-tier municipal council is the approving body, frequently delegating approval authority to a "committee of adjustment" or a "land-division committee." Because the land-severance application is reviewed in the context of the municipality's planning policies and regulations, to which the public has already had input, there is no requirement for public notice. The approving body does have the option to give notice to people who could be affected by the application (adjacent landowners). If you hear about a severance application that might affect a natural area, you can write to the municipal clerk and approving body and state your concerns, as well as ask for notice of the final decision. If you have requested and received such notice, you can appeal the decision to the OMB.

Inappropriate development through plans of subdivision and random severancing poses a major threat to wetlands and woodlands.

Plan of subdivision approval traditionally has been the responsibility of MMAH. However, with recent changes to the Planning Act, subdivision approval has been delegated to regional municipalities. Some counties and lower-tier municipalities have also been granted responsibility for approving plans of subdivision in their jurisdictions. Also, amendments to the Planning Act that will come into effect in 1996 name as approval authorities for plans of subdivision the counties of Bruce, Grey, Hastings, Huron, Lambton, Peterborough, Prince Edward, Victoria and Wellington. Find out from your municipal clerk if your municipality has approval authority for plans of subdivision.

Municipalities do not have to give notice of subdivision proposals. However, some municipalities may give general notice or at least require that a sign be posted on the property of the proposed subdivision. A public meeting is not required for a plan of subdivision, although some municipalities hold them as a matter of course.

The approval authority, whether it be lower tier, upper tier or the MMAH, may either draft approve or turn down the proposed plan of subdivision. Appeals to the OMB on a plan of subdivision must be made before draft approval is given. To be able to influence this planning process, citizens have to keep a very close eye on what the municipality is doing. Plans of subdivision often are approved unnoticed by the public at large.

Environmental Advisory Committees

In some municipalities, citizen or environmental or ecological advisory committees work with municipal councils to evaluate the impacts of development on the local environment and can act as custodians of the inventory of natural heritage features and areas. Environmental and Ecological Advisory Committees (EEACs) can also provide useful forums for communication between councils, planning departments, citizens and landowners.

Most EEACs have similar goals and terms of reference. If your municipality has no EEAC, contact a neighbouring municipality or town that has a successful and independant EEAC, and ask a member to discuss their role with you and your municipal council. Encourage the council to establish a local EEAC in your area to give them advice on local environmental matters.

When a wetland or woodland is under immediate threat

The tools described above are alternatives for influencing the planning process for the protection of wetlands and woodlands in your area. But how about when a wetland or woodland is under immediate threat by a development proposal?

You have to get involved right away. Your chances of helping to save the area decrease the further along the development proposal is. As already stated, with recent changes to the Planning Act, the opportunity to appeal decisions has been restricted. You cannot appeal council decisions if you were not involved in the consultation process.

Many citizens have successfully fought development proposals and organized their communities to do the same. Jim Richards is one of these people.

PROFILE

Jim Richards

e's greying at the temples now, but for Jim Richards, the memories of school days spent exploring the Oshawa Second Marsh remain vivid. "I remember putting sealer-jar rings around my pant legs to keep the leeches off," he says with a chuckle. "I thought it was a hell of a great spot." He looks over the marsh and adds, "I still do, despite all the abuse it has taken."

Jim Richards's story is one of perseverance writ large: he has fought for the integrity of the Oshawa Second Marsh for close to 30 years. In the course of the campaign, his name has become synonymous with wetland conservation.

It all began modestly, Jim recalls. Anticipating a boom in ship traffic after the opening of the St. Lawrence Seaway, the Oshawa Harbour Commission announced that it would be expanding the port. Then the other shoe dropped: rather than expanding the existing port, the commission proposed to create an enormous new one by destroying Second Marsh. Jim was convinced it was a misunderstanding, that the planners simply didn't grasp what was at stake and how rich and diverse and important the marsh was.

"I was a shy kid and didn't really know anybody of influence", Jim notes, but his passion for the marsh was such that he felt he had to act. Calling around to naturalist and hunter-and-angler clubs, Jim urged attendance at a meeting to plan a response. "There were three of us at the first meeting, and the next week there were five," he recalls. The plan remained simple: approach the council and show them that what the harbour commission was planning was unconscionable.

"After we gave our speech to council, I realized we were getting the brush-off," Jim says. But he was not about to go away. "I had a personal resolve. I just said, 'No, you are not going to destroy that marsh.' My friends said I shouldn't commit so heavily, that I might lose, but I'd say, 'No, that's not going to happen.'"

The first few years of the campaign to save the marsh were "really rough," Jim admits. "In the early days, we got beat constantly," and the inclination to just walk away was always there. But with experience came contacts and an understanding of how to deal with the media.

KEITH DISCIPLINE

I had a personal resolve. I just said, 'No, you are not going to destroy that marsh.'

"Throughout the '70s and '80s we sent out press releases every week, and if we didn't, the papers would call us," he relates. Jim was good copy: a sharp tongue combined with an encyclopedic knowledge of the issues made him a tough opponent. He had also cultivated contacts in every level of government and found many sympathetic bureaucrats who could discreetly help the cause. "I used to get stuff in plain brown envelopes from the public-works department all the time," he says with a laugh.

In 1976, Jim formalized his involvement in the issue by establishing the Second Marsh Defence Association. The group's subsequent success, he believes, was due to the broad spectrum of its membership (the executive combined members of local naturalist and hunting-and-fishing clubs), a high level of organization, and its ability to reach out to the membership of organizations such as the FON and local clubs for help.

And just as it would welcome any help it could get, so would the association lend a hand on other wetland causes where it could. "I looked at the marsh as symbolic of other wetlands," Jim explains, and that meant getting involved in such things such as the campaign for a provincial wetlands policy.

In late 1992, the ownership of Second Marsh was transferred back to a conservation-minded Oshawa City Council from the harbour commission, and Jim Richards and the by-then Friends of Second Marsh began planning a major rehabilitation effort for the wetland.

As he watches a northern harrier drift over a section of reclaimed marsh, Jim contemplates his motivation for sticking with such a long-drawn-out and often highly personal campaign. "As an individual and a naturalist I could not just stand by." He adds, "I had already gotten so much from my association with things wild that I had to put something back."

Then the ever-restless Jim Richards jumps up and points across the marsh to a piece of property still owned by the harbour commission. "I want that hill," he states bluntly, and something tells you there are more sleepless nights in store for powers that be in Oshawa.

Environmental advocacy

You have just realized that a favourite wetland or woodland will soon cease to exist. Fast action is needed to save the area. What do you do? Below are the important steps you should take.

1) Find out who is doing what and why.

Call your municipal clerk and/or planner. Make sure that these questions are answered:

◆ What type of development is proposed?

◆ Has the development proposal been given the go-ahead?

◆ Is an official-plan amendment needed?

◆ What is the current zoning and is a new zoning by-law or amendment needed?

◆ Has there or will there be a public meeting?

◆ Does the natural area have any status (ESA, provincially significant ANSI, etc.)?

◆ Do wetlands or woodlands have any protection afforded to them in the official plan?

Other useful legislation for environmental protection

The Planning Act and its land-use policies are particularly important in determining the shape of a community over the long term. However, there are other pieces of legislation that can be used to influence local environmental decisions and local resource management (see Useful Documents at back of chapter).

Municipal Act
Authorizes municipalities to adopt tree by-laws and site alteration by-laws to control tree cutting and pre-development site grading and alteration.

Endangered Species Act
Prohibits interference with species regulated as endangered, and their habitats.

Fisheries Act
Prohibits harmful alteration, disruption or destruction of any fish habitat.

Conservation Land Act
Authorizes the Conservation Land Tax Reduction Program, which rebates property owners' taxes for provincially significant wetlands, ANSIs, areas zoned Escarpment Natural, and nongovernment conservation agency nature reserves.

Conservation Authorities Act
Authorizes regulation of filling or excavating in valleylands and floodplains ("cut and fill" regulations).

Trees Act
Authorizes municipalities to adopt by-laws to control tree-cutting.

Topsoil Preservation Act
Authorizes municipalities to control removal of topsoil during development. In 1993, less than 10% of rural municipalities had passed by-laws.

Environmental Assessment Act
Requires impact assessments and consideration of alternatives to all public-sector activities unless they are exempted from the environmental assessment process.

Crown Forest Sustainability Act
Broad new legislation requiring, among many other matters, that all forest management activities on provincially-owned lands be governed by formal forest management plans.

Game and Fish Act
Among many matters, authorizes the creation and management of wildlife management areas, regulates wildlife management, and protects numerous non-game species.

◆ Has the official plan been updated to take into consideration the new policy statements?

◆ Are there any government reports, consultant studies or municipal documents on the development proposal or the natural area? Can you get copies or take a look at them at the municipal office?

◆ When can you come in to look at the official plan and zoning by-laws?

◆ Will the clerk arrange to notify you of any municipal action affecting this area?

Call your local MNR office and ask staff:

◆ Do they know anything about the proposed development?

◆ What is the MNR's position on the proposal?

If the area affected is a wetland:

◆ Is the wetland provincially significant (Class 1—3)?

◆ Is it regionally or locally significant (Class 4—7)?

◆ Has the wetland been evaluated? If not, will it be evaluated before approval for the development proposal is considered?

If the area is a woodland or other natural area:

◆ Have any studies or evaluations been conducted in the area?

◆ Is it an ANSI? Is it a significant woodland, valleyland, or fish or wildllife habitat?

◆ Is it habitat for endangered or threatened species, or any other species at risk?

◆ Are there any reports or studies available for the area?

Call the CA and pose the same questions you asked the MNR, as well as:

◆ Are there any watershed/subwatershed studies of this area?

◆ Are there any intentions to undertake these studies? Why?

◆ Is the site a significant valleyland? Do they know of any significant species or habitats there?

2) Evaluate your information and get more.

Compare what the MNR, CA and municipality told you. Take a look at the material available.

◆ If the wetland or woodland is significant, is the municipality giving it proper consideration?

◆ Are the policy statements being complied with?

◆ Is the municipality, MNR or CA overlooking something?

Get more information. Contact the local naturalist club, environmental groups, provincial organizations like the FON, or the Natural Heritage Information Centre.

◆ Do they know what is going on?

◆ Do they have records or inventories for the site?

◆ Is there anything significant that the municipality, CA or MNR overlooked?

◆ Do they want to help save the area? What can they do to help?

3) Plan a strategy to save the wetland or woodland.

Write a letter to the municipality immediately and express your concerns, even if they are not detailed. You can always write a follow-up letter later, by yourself or as part of a group. Remember to always ask questions in your letter. This way the party you are writing to will have to respond.

Find out who your allies are.

◆ Inform your neighbours.

◆ Contact other groups (ratepayers, anglers and hunters, local university or college).

◆ Approach local politicians (ones likely to support you).

Hold a meeting.

◆ Examine your opportunities for approaching the municipal council.

◆ Decide on an approach or approaches, such as:

a) presentations and submissions to council;

b) letter campaign;

c) support from provincial groups;

d) when to write to appropriate ministries, ministers (for pointers on how to write to a minister see Appendix—The Game of Letters);

e) when to go to the media and how (for pointers on how to write a news release see Appendix—Writing a News Release);

f) getting broader community support;

g) the possibility of acquiring the land;

h) the need for a lawyer.

◆ Find out what expertise and connections your group has.

◆ If a municipal election is on the horizon, look at the possibility of getting your own candidate on council.

◆ Assign people specific responsibilities.

◆ Think about creating a formal group to save the natural area (friends of ...).

◆ Be prepared for a fight.

Try to keep the pressure on.

◆ Keep focused on your goal.

◆ Be creative and keep reevaluating your strategy.

◆ If one approach isn't working, try something else.

◆ Be professional, even if things get nasty.

◆ Don't get sidetracked. Once you start a dozen other related projects will come up.

The Niagara Escarpment: a unique natural environment with its own land-use system

Development interests on the escarpment are strong, whether they be for gravel extraction, golf courses, ski hills or more housing.

The Niagara Escarpment is the only area in Ontario that has a special land-use plan. The Niagara Escarpment Plan (NEP) came into effect in 1985 to protect the escarpment's natural environment from development pressures. This mandate is spelled out in the Niagara Escarpment Planning and Development Act, which was created ('to provide for the maintenance of the Niagara Escarpment and the land in its vicinity substantially as a continuous natural environment and to ensure only such development occurs as is compatible with that environment.')

The escarpment, a 450-million-year-old landform, stretches 725 km in Ontario, from Niagara Falls to Tobermory. The area within the plan, 1,830 square kilometres, cuts across eight regions and counties. The Niagara Escarpment Commission (NEC) oversees the implementation of the NEP along the escarpment. Major decisions are made by the NEC board, which has 17 members. Nine members are appointees of the MOEE, and eight represent the municipalities.

The Niagara Escarpment Plan has two main thrusts: first, protection and enhancement of the natural areas, associated landscapes and cultural features; and second, concentration of intrusive development in areas where it poses the least threat to the environment. To achieve the intent of the act and plan, the Niagara Escarpment Plan Area has been divided into seven zones: Escarpment Natural, Escarpment Protection, Escarpment Rural, Minor Urban Centre, Urban, Escarpment Recreation and Mineral Resource Extraction.

Escarpment Natural, Escarpment Protection and Escarpment Rural areas are protected from intrusive development in varying degrees, with most protection afforded to Escarpment Natural areas. Within these sections, development is controlled by the NEC through a building-permit system. The NEC board decides what developments are suitable and in conformity with the NEP.

There has been vocal opposition to the NEC and NEP from the time they were put in place. Development interests on the escarpment are strong, whether they be for gravel extraction, golf courses, ski hills or more housing. In addition, lobbying against the NEP based on the premise of property rights is ever present. Today, opposition to the NEP remains significant. If we hope to retain the Niagara Escarpment Planning and Development Act and the NEP in the long term our voices must be heard. If you live on the escarpment or are interested in its future, you should vocally support the Niagara Escarpment Plan whenever possible. Keep abreast of what is going on. The FON will continue to provide updates on the escarpment issue whenever necessary via *Seasons* magazine, but individual letters, phone calls and visits with MPPs are the most powerful protective measures that exist.

Many people over the years have fought for the protection of the Niagara Escarpment. However, it is fair to say that none have been able to match the determination and passion of Lyn MacMillan. Her continued work for the preservation of the escarpment is undoubtedly one of the reasons the NEP is in place today.

PROFILE

Lyn MacMillan

here are probably more than a few provincial bureacrats, political aides and politicians, current and former, who have strong recollections of dealing with Lyn MacMillan. As leader of the Coalition on the Niagara Escarpment (CONE) for five years in the late '70s and early '80s, Lyn turned her laser-sharp attention on the province's political leadership — particularly then-premier Bill Davis —to demand enlightened treatment for what she saw as one of the province's natural treasures.

Her task began simply enough with a phone call from the FON, requesting assistance on the issue of preservation of the escarpment. Lyn already had a soft spot for the escarpment: almost every weekend her family would explore sections of the Bruce Trail. "It was a great way to exhaust five rambunctious kids," she explains.

After delving into the issue, Lyn saw the need for a coalition and drew together seven groups, including the FON, to form CONE. The groups, which had similar views, combined to share resources and membership interest. "We had one thing in mind," Lyn notes, "and that was to keep the Niagara Escarpment Planning and Development Act and Commission going and to get an orderly plan out." At the time, she explains, municipalities and some ratepayer groups along the escarpment were vociferously opposing the province's attempt to take control of helter-skelter development and aggregate extraction in the sensitive escarpment environment.

But while the goals of CONE may have seemed straightforward to Lyn, her advocacy efforts at first drew little interest at Queen's Park. Then, she recalls, still somewhat amazed at

To be a successful lobbyist, Lyn learned, you have to know your facts inside out, understand any laws or policies that apply to your situation and never say anything you can not support with facts.

CONE's good fortune, the government made "a big mistake" — the minister of housing, ignoring advice from all sides, approved the building of an "enormous executive retreat" in a prominent escarpment location. Lyn stoked the fires as the press dissected the issue for six straight weeks.

If they didn't realize it then, what the politicians eventually discovered was that this was only the beginning of their dealings with CONE and Lyn MacMillan. "They underestimate your staying power," she notes. But there were also plenty of frustrating days when quitting looked very attractive. "On those days," Lyn says, "I would get a good book, go to bed early. The next morning there would be a cheque in the mail, or I'd have a bright idea, or some influential person would come along."

To be a successful lobbyist, she learned, you have to know your facts inside out, understand any laws or policies that apply to your situation and never say anything you can not support with facts. Then, she says, "Go to the top."

On hot political issues, Lyn believes there is little point in dealing with midlevel bureaucrats. When the timing was right and the moment merited it, she would get in to see the minister, or better yet, the premier. "I was always very polite and very brief, "she states, but, in her crisp fashion, she was always direct. "I would just keep reminding them of their responsibilities. I would say, 'You made the law, you set up the commission, I'm just reminding you of the promises you made.'"

Lyn admits that she found tasks such as holding news conferences and meeting with the premier intimidating at first. Her daughter helped her relax in front of the press by sug-

KEVIN KAVANAUGH

gesting she approach the situation as if she were talking the issue over with a friend. For meeting the premier, Lyn prepared herself by asking, "Who pays his salary?" and reiterating to herself, "I'm his equal and I won't be pushed around."

CONE did not concentrate all its efforts at Queen's Park. Raising awareness and appreciation for the escarpment among the public was also an important part of the coalition's work. "I talked to dozens of groups and got them to write letters that proved very useful in turning the tide," Lyn recalls. "You always have to be extremely polite and friendly with supporters and you have to exude confidence about eventual success," she adds, noting that CONE relied almost entirely on small donations from individuals for funding.

Looking back, Lyn says she feels the key was to take things one step at a time and not to get overwhelmed by the big picture. "The process is analogous to reading a book, — you keep turning the pages and suddenly you've reached the end."

A strong sense of conviction also helps. "I'm a great believer in getting out there and getting into the act", Lyn says. even if that just means writing a letter. You can sit back in sadness or you can say, 'They are not going to drain our wetlands, they are not going to destroy our woodlots.' You put up a fight."

Information sources

Government agencies

For information on general inquiries, government bookstores, municipalities, MNR and CAs. See Information Sources, on page 20.

NEC
232 Guelph Street
Georgetown, Ontario
L7G 4B1
The NEC can be contacted at (905) 877-5191.

Nongovernment agencies

Canadian Environmental Law Association
517 College Street, Suite 401,
Toronto, Ontario, M6G 4H2
(416) 960-2284

Canadian Institute for Environmental Law and Policy,
517 College Street, Suite 400,
Toronto, Ontario M6G 4A2
(416) 923-3529

Planning documents

Planning Act
The Planning Act can be obtained from any of the government bookstores, see Information Sources , page 20.

Proposed Policy Statement and *Implementation Guidelines*
These documents can be obtained from any government bookstore or from the Communications Branch of the MMAH, (416)585-7041.

Communications Branch
MMAH
17th Floor, 777 Bay Street
Toronto, Ontario M5G 2E5

Ministry of Municipal Affairs and Housing *A Citizen's Guide Series* to:
#1 The Planning Act
#2 Official Plans
#3 Zoning By-laws
#4 Subdivisions
#5 Land Severance
#6 Ontario Municipal Board
#7 Northern Ontario
#8 Building Permits

This series is available from the Program Services Branch of MMAH, (416) 585-6244.

Program Services Branch
MMAH
13th Floor, 777 Bay Street
Toronto, Ontario
M5G 2E5

Useful documents

Government documents

Brownell, Vivian R. and Brendon M.H. Larson. 1995. *An Evaluation Framework for Natural Areas in the Regional Municipality of Ottawa-Carleton. Volume 1.* Regional Municipality of Ottawa-Carleton. Ottawa

Department of Fisheries and Oceans. 1986. *Policy for the management of fish habitat.* Ottawa

Doering, R.L., et al. 1991. *Planning for sustainability: towards integrating environmental protection into land-use planning.* Publication #12. Royal Commission on the Future of the Toronto Waterfront. Toronto

Gartner Lee. 1993. *A Greenlands System for York Region: Final Draft Report.* Regional Municipality of York. Newmarket

Geomatics. 1993. *Natural Heritage System for the Oak Ridges Moraine Area: GTA Portion. Background Study No. 4.* Oak Ridges Moraine Technical Working Committee. Toronto

Gore and Storrie Limited. 1993. *Town of Markham Natural Features Study: Phase 2 Implementation Plan.* Gore and Storrie Limited. Markham

Hough Woodland Naylor Dance Limited and Gore and Storrie Ltd. 1995. *Restoring Natural Habitats.* Waterfront Regeneration Trust. Toronto

Ministry of the Environment and Energy. 1994. *Water management: policies, guidelines, provincial water-quality objectives of the Ministry of Environment and Energy.* Toronto

Ministry of the Environment and Energy and Ministry of Natural Resources. 1993. *Water Management on a Watershed Basis: implementing an ecosystems approach.* Toronto

Ministry of the Environment and Energy and Ministry of Natural Resources. 1993. *Subwatershed planning.* Toronto

Ministry of the Environment and Energy and Ministry of Natural Resources. 1993. *Integrating water management objectives into municipal planning documents.* Toronto

Ministry of Natural Resources. 1987. *Implementation Strategy: Areas of Natural and Scientific Interest.* Provincial Parks and Natural Heritage Policy Branch. Toronto

Oak Ridges Moraine Technical Working Committee. 1994. *Oak Ridges Moraine Strategy for the Greater Toronto Area: An Ecosystem Approach for Long Term Protection and Management.* Ministry of Natural Resources. Toronto

Metropolitan Toronto and Region Conservation Authority. 1992. *Valley and Stream Corridor Management Program.* Toronto

Royal Commission on the Future of the Toronto Waterfront. 1992. *Regeneration. Toronto's Waterfront and the Sustainable City: Final Report.* Queen's Printer of Ontario. Toronto

Tomalty, Ray, Robert B. Gibson, Donald H.M. Alexander and John Fisher. 1994. *Ecosystem Planning for Canadian Urban Regions.* ICURR Publications. Toronto

Waterfront Regeneration Trust. 1995. *Lake Ontario Greenway Strategy.* Waterfront Regeneration Trust. Toronto

Nongovernment documents

Estrin, David and John Swaigen. 1993. *Environment on Trial: A guide to Ontario Environmental Law and Policy.* Edmond Montgomery Publications Limited. Toronto

Tip of the Mitt Watershed Council. 1992. *Michigan Wetlands: Yours to Protect. A Citizen's Guide to Local Involvement in Wetland Protection.* Tip of the Mitt Watershed Council. Michigan (P.O. Box 300, Conway, Michigan, 49722. USA)

CHAPTER THREE

Protecting Private Lands

Land Acquisition & Stewardship

BY JANE ROOTS

hapter three reviews the array of tools for land acquisition and stewardship that can be used to protect wetlands and woodlands in Ontario. Experiences of people who have been involved in land acquisition and stewardship are related.

Also included is a hypothetical case study that illustrates how and when the tools can be applied. It outlines five private properties within which a wetland/woodland complex is found. Each property has distinct physical characteristics and varying natural significance, and would require a slightly different approach to meet conservation objectives. The scenario presented should provide some ideas on the opportunities available through land acquisition and stewardship for the protection of wetlands and woodlands.

Implementation of tools that will be outlined demands a long-term commitment from a conservation group. Successful protection of natural habitats through land acquisition or stewardship requires ongoing work. If a group acquires a property, at the very least some minimal maintenance will always be needed, and in some cases more-intensive management of the site. For land stewardship, it is critical to include a long-term monitoring component. Details on how to organize and sustain a group in order to acquire and manage land, or implement land-stewardship techniques, is addressed in the companion document *Creative Conservation: A Handbook for Ontario Land Trusts.*

Using land-acquisition tools, your group will ultimately own property, while with land-stewardship techniques you will encourage private landowners to protect their own natural areas. These are two different approaches to protecting land. Mac Kirk, a longtime conservationist profiled here, has a definite opinion on which approach he prefers.

PROFILE

Malcolm Kirk

o Malcolm Kirk's way of thinking, nothing beats acquisition when it comes to protection of ecologically sensitive areas. And Mac understands all the blood, sweat and fine print that approach entails — he has been involved in the purchase of dozens of important sites, including Dorcas Bay and Petrel Point on behalf of the FON.

But he acknowledges that acquisition of land today is a much tougher conservation prescription than it was even a decade ago. "The trouble is that after the land boom of the '80s, prices fell only slightly and then plateaued. They're not going up any more, but they're not going down, either," he says, "and both public and private sources of funds are decreasing."

There is definitely a role to be played by land-stewardship programs. The only drawback is that stewardship does not offer the "guaranteed continuity" that acquisition does, he notes. Subsequent owners of lands now in steward-ship may be "totally hostile" to conservation or may need the cash that development might bring.

Mac himself worked for 16 years, from 1957 to 1973, as resources manager with the Grey Sauble Conservation Authority, a job he calls "the best in the province." During his time with the authority, he managed an active acquisition program that targeted wetlands, headwater areas and stream corridors.

The key to the success of the program, and of purchases made independently on behalf of the FON, he says, was the federation and its local agent being well known in the community. If a farmer had a marsh he was willing to sell, he knew who to call. Similarly, if an orchid bog on the Bruce Peninsula was up for sale, Mac was bound to hear about it, and just as likely to have already had some contact with the owners. He also made sure there was broad-based community support for protection: "I spent about 40 nights a year out with slides, selling conservation to the grass roots."

But while the days of acquiring wetland areas for $10 an acre are probably gone forever, Mac believes that with a little creativity, important natural areas can still be acquired. The two biggest allies in the acquisition of wetlands today, for example, are the Provincial Wetlands Policy and flood-and-fill

regulations. A developer, Mac explains, may think the piece of marsh he owns is worth $1 million for housing, but if he can be convinced of the hurdles he must overcome to develop the property, it may be worth only $100,000. "Once you peel him off the ceiling," Mac says with a laugh, "you can negotiate."

Once again, Mac Kirk speaks from experience. With the Beaver Valley Heritage Society in the mid '80s, he was involved in convincing a developer that land he had acquired would never get the desired development approvals. The developer ended up donating the parcel to the Ontario Heritage Foundation. "He was probably glad he did before the recession hit," Mac adds.

But any time actual cash will be changing hands, he says, obtaining a formal, independent evaluation of the land's worth is critical. An official appraisal has its uses: it gives you a fixed target for fundraising, for one thing. "You can go to people and say 'just this amount will put us over the top.'" And maybe it will serve as a negotiating tool with the landowner as well.

Mac acknowledges that one of the more difficult aspects of a purchase can be what to do with the property afterwards. If the area is remote and in good natural condition, then it can easily be left alone. But more accessible or degraded sites may need money and management, and to that end, he sees potential in the concept of locally administered land trusts.

Currently, Mac is involved in establishing the Blue Mountain Watershed Trust for the area around Collingwood. "People will respond to local projects" with cheques, he explains, and he has his sales pitch ready: "People come up here to escape the horrors of the big city, but development can turn this area into another Scarborough. How would you like to help us preserve some natural heritage to maintain the quality of rural life that you value?"

Local school children discover a natural ice-cave deep in Feversham Gorge. The gorge was purchased by the Grey-Sauble Conservation Authority with funds raised by the Senior League Endowment Society of Collingwood.

Land acquisition and stewardship tools

There are a variety of tools that people like Mac Kirk have used, with the support of conservation groups, to protect land in private hands. Outlined below are the main land acquisition and stewardship methods your group can use to protect wetlands and woodlands.

Land acquisition tools

Land purchase

An outright purchase of land is referred to as a fee-simple-interest real-estate transaction. It is the most common process for acquiring land and provides the owner with the most control over the property. As long as activities on the property are within the law, the owner can determine how the land will be used, who can enter, and how and when the land can be sold.

First right-of-refusal (to purchase) agreement

If the landowner is not willing or able to sell the property right away, it may be possible to obtain a first-right-of-refusal agreement, which means that if and when the owner does decide to sell, the holder of the agreement (your organization, for example) would have the first chance to purchase the land.

Option to purchase

An option to purchase is a legally binding agreement designed to facilitate the purchase of property at a predetermined price before a specified date. It can be effectively used as an interim control while your group raises the funds to make the purchase.

Life estate

This involves the direct purchase of land (acquiring fee-simple interest) with conditions. As an example, the vendors and/or their heirs may retain the right to live on the property for the rest of their lives. This land-acquisition process is rarely used in Ontario.

Donation

A donation comprises an outright gift of a property. Conditions may be attached to the donation— for example, that trails be kept up or that family members be allowed to remove some firewood from the property. The value of a donation is determined by an independent appraisal undertaken by a registered appraiser. Depending on the landowners' restrictions on the use of land, their income-tax status and the availability of capital-gains exemptions, a value less than the fair market one can be chosen. There are significant income-tax implications related to donations. Always ask landowners to consult with their own tax advisers regarding what is best for them.

When the 1995 federal budget was announced, changes to the Income Tax Act were proposed to facilitate donations of ecologically sensitive land. When such land was donated to an environmental charity under the old system, the amount claimed for the donation was limited to 20% of the individual's or corporation's annual net income. Donors were able to carry unused claims forward for up to five years, helping them maximize deductions. However, when the value of the land donated was high relative to the donor's income, the 20% limit hampered donations. 100% of the value of land donations can now be claimed against net income.

Bargain sale

When landowners are ready to sell, they may be in a position to consider a bargain sale—a combined donation and sale. The value of the property is established through an appraisal, then the property is sold to a charitable organization for less than the appraised value. The difference between the appraised fair-market value and the actual purchase price is considered a donation. Depending on the landowners' financial situation, a bargain sale may be able to save them capital-gains taxes, as well as provide a tax credit.

Part purchase

This is a direct purchase under fee-simple transaction arrangements for a part of the property. Severancing of the property is usually required before a part purchase. For this reason many conservation organizations are hesitant to use this tool. Currently the Crown and conservation authorities are exempt from severance restrictions.

Purchase and leaseback

This method involves fee-simple acquisition of property and subsequent leasing of all or a portion of the property for a specific purpose (such as farming). Specific instructions or restrictions on the use of the property being leased can be given. Purchase and leaseback is a very useful technique when you want to secure a property immediately and allow the former owners access to the property.

Purchase and sale back

Similar to purchase and leaseback above, this requires acquisition of title and the subsequent sale back, with restrictive covenants on the title to protect certain features. A portion of the property may be sold through a severance. This portion may include buildings or features that are not related to the objectives of the project.

*Land
stewardship
tools*

Stewardship agreement

A stewardship agreement between your organization and a landowner can be made to maintain a wetland or woodland on the property. Agreements can be written or verbal and rely on trust between partners. A written agreement can be a formal or informal document that outlines what the landowner will or will not do on the property or portion thereof. Written agreements are a positive first step in the long-term management of an area targeted for protection. Very detailed agreements are often based on a management plan for the property. Agreements are generally set up for a specified period of time and may be renewed subject to mutual consent.

Management plans

Management plans are developed with a private landowner to maintain a wetland or woodland on the property. Depending on the detail desired and the relative experience of people in your organization, it may be necessary to bring in experts in ecology, forestry or wildlife management. MNR or CA staff may be able to help you, although staff people with expertise in these areas are in short supply. An alternative is to hire a consultant. It is important that the management plan for the portion of the wetland or woodland located on the property not be in conflict with the management interests for the entire property.

Lease

A lease is an interest in land for a defined period of time wherein the landowner grants to the tenant the exclusive possession of the property in exchange for rent. This means that the tenant has absolute control over the property during the term of the lease, even priority over the landlord, provided that conditions specified in the lease are observed. A lease is temporary, although it may be renewed for successive periods of less than 21 years. The conditions of the lease required by the property owner may pose limitations on the use and development of the property. Leases are used extensively in agriculture and for urban property.

Conservation easement

A conservation easement is a voluntary agreement between a landowner and a conservation body to "conserve, maintain, restore or enhance" the natural features of a property by placing conditions on its management. For example, the agreement could spell out how a woodlot is to be managed. The specific conditions of an easement are decided by the landowner and conservation body. The easement is registered on the title of the property and binds the present owner and all future owners to the terms of the agreement. A conservation easement does not give the easement holder title to the property. For landowners, a conservation easement is a way to protect the special attributes of their property, while retaining ownership.

This new tool became available in 1995, when the Conservation Lands Act was revised to allow private landowners to enter into conservation easements with charitable conservation organizations, municipal councils, native bands and conservation authorities. Prior to this, landowners could enter into conservation easements only with the Crown and its agencies. To date this new tool has not been used by any conservation group, but it is being reviewed extensively.

Summary of alternatives

It is important to keep in mind that the land acquisition and stewardship tools outlined above vary in several fundamental ways, such as:

◆ the strength of protection they offer;

◆ the duration of protection they offer;

◆ the degree to which they restrict rights;

◆ the speed with which they can be applied;

◆ the cost of implementation.

Each of these factors influences the technique your group will choose. It is important to be able to mesh your objectives with those of the landowner, as well as with your own financial situation. Table 2 provides an estimation of the time needed, cost in year of publication and protection strength of each tool. Please refer to the category descriptions following the table.

Table 2: Land Acquisition and Stewardship Tools

TOOL	PROTECTION LEVEL	PERSON DAYS	TIME FRAME IN DAYS	LAND COST PER ACRE	RELATED COST
Fee-Simple Purchase	High	6	90 — 120	a) $400 b) $800 c) $1200 d) $1800 e) $2200	$6000
First Right of Refusal	Low	4	15 30	NA	$2500
Option to Purchase	Low	4	30 — 45	NA	$2500
Life Estate	High	10	90 — 120	a) $400 b) $800 c) $1200 d) $1800	$6000
Donation	High	8	180 — 270	NA	$6000
Bargain Sale	High	9	180 — 270	a) $400 b) $800 c) $1200 d) $1800	$6000
Part Purchase	High	9	120 — 180	a) $400 b) $800 c) $1200 d) $1800	$6000

Table 2: Land Acquisition and Stewardship Tools continued

TOOL	PROTECTION LEVEL	PERSON DAYS	TIME FRAME IN DAYS	LAND COST PER ACRE	RELATED COST
Purchase and Leaseback	Medium	10	90 —120	a) $400 b) $800 c) $1200 d) $1800	$6000
Purchase and Sale Back	Medium	10	120 — 270	a) $400 b) $800 c) $1200 d) $1800	$6000
Stewardship Agreement	Medium	9	30 —90	a) $10 b) $20 c) $40 d) $60	$2500
Lease	Medium	5	30 — 90	a) $20 b) $40 c) $75 d) $150	$2500
Conservation Easement	High	14	120 — 270	a) $0 b) $25 c) $50 d) $100	$6000

Description of Categories from William B. Sargant. Workshop notes prepared for Workshop on Protecting Wetlands and Woodlands, Orillia, Ontario. November 9, 1992

Protection level

High The use of tools that result in control of the property by the conservation organization are considered to achieve a high level of protection.

Medium The use of tools in this category generally result in temporary protection and/or in less-than-complete control of the property.

Low These tools generally provide interim and limited control of properties. Implementation is less costly and makes available the time for pursuing medium-or-high-protection options.

Person days

This is an estimate of the time required to implement the technique—to contact and meet the landowner, visit the site, arrange for an appraisal, negotiate the agreement, coordinate funding approval and legal work, and follow up once the transaction has been completed. The work may be spread over a considerable period, involving anything from half a day to an hour or so here and there.

Time frame

This is an estimate of the range of time needed to fully implement the tools, including contacting the landowner, securing an appraisal, negotiating an agreement, releasing funding and undertaking survey and legal work. It is critical to be able to meet the time frame of the landowner or at least advise the landowner of the time required, to alleviate false expectations. If everything goes smoothly and the cash is in place, a purchase could be completed in 10 to15 days, whereas a purchase or donation involving a life estate and endowment with complex tax implications may require several years or more to complete.

The estimates are based on the experience of the Nature Conservancy of Canada. Allow for extra time if your legal firm is not used to dealing with land transactions of this nature.

Land cost per acre

The following are average costs of land for various habitats. Prices, based on 1996 figures, are influenced by market conditions, location, official-plan and zoning by-law designations, access, presence of buildings, major natural features and other considerations. Parcels adjacent to each other may vary in value by as much as several hundred dollars.

Market value is ultimately determined in the marketplace by willing vendors and purchasers. Put simply, land is worth what someone is willing to pay for it.

The following designations refer to the average land values listed in the table.

a) Interior properties with no or limited access and no other values (e.g., timber, river frontage).
b) Properties with access and no other values.
c) Properties with good access and some other values (e.g., agriculture).
d) Properties with good access and several other values (e.g., agriculture and improvements).
e) Properties with good access, superior or location (e.g., paved road) and superior attributes (lakefront) or improvements (house/cottage).

Related costs

These include appraisal, survey, legal fees, document preparation (e.g. licence agreement) and special studies (e.g. environmental audit of property).

Volunteers at work on FON's Crozier Nature Reserve.

If landowners appear to be unreceptive when contacted don't be disillusioned. Over time your work will pay off as they become more comfortable with environmental suggestions.

Contact with private landowners

In implementing the majority of land acquisition and stewardship tools, contact with private landowners will be necessary. You may decide to focus on one "core" area, or just monitor the area for threats or changes in land use. If you do choose to pursue a more active course, you will need to consider how you will approach landowners. Take time before you do to think about the best way to introduce your ideas to them.

An integral part of any contact is educating landowners about the natural values of their property and increasing awareness of the importance of long-term commitment to a healthy, diverse landscape.

Things to think about when seeing a landowner:

◆ relax and listen;

◆ try to find common grounds for conversation;

◆ be observant and know something about the area and the person's property;

◆ make clear your position as a liaison for your organization;

◆ don't raise false expectations, underpromise or overdeliver;

◆ remember, people give to people, not to faceless organizations;

◆ remember, people protect land, not legal text on a piece of paper;

◆ know why you want to protect the land and be able to explain it in a variety of ways;

◆ recognize and honestly admit that funds are limited (that yours is a non-profit organization);

◆ try to avoid talking price; instead talk about interests in the property, both the landowner's and those of your organization;

◆ try to overcome resistance with options, patience and a willingness to understand where the landowner is coming from;

◆ if the landowner doesn't want to do anything, leave him/her alone;

◆ be prepared to say no and walk away; often the landowner is testing you and will choose to come back and talk.

Once initial visits with the landowner have been completed, you and your organization will have a better idea of what steps to take next in working towards the protection of specific natural areas. Establish what tools and techniques can be used to protect the area in ways that meet your groups' objectives and are compatible with the landowner's wishes and desires.

Woodpecker Woods and Wetlands

hen and how should your group apply certain tools? Using the hypothetical case study of Woodpecker Woods and Wetlands, we will take you through some of the situations and opportunities your group may encounter.

Woodpecker Woods and Wetlands is a 150-hectare (370-acre) forest-and-swamp complex containing 64 hectares (170 acres) of a mixed-age deciduous forest community, with some uncommon and rare species for this part of Ontario (Carolinian species at the northern edge of their range). The swamp is on the southwestern edge of the forest and contains Cedar Pond, a 10-acre pond fed by Muskrat Creek, a cold-water stream. The woods and wetland are located in a mixed-farming region of Ontario, approximately an hours drive from a large urban area. (Please refer to the map on the next page.)

The woodland is isolated and has seen some selective harvesting in the past. Its ecological value is still high, given the disappearance of most other woods in the area. Woodpecker Woods is popular with local naturalists, although access is relatively restricted. Both the creek and the marsh around the pond are in good condition, with a mixture of native flora and fauna typical of this part of southern Ontario. The marsh is a good birding area in the spring.

The surrounding land is being used for a mixture of farming and rural-residential housing. To the east and south of the woodland are midsized dairy and market farms that are doing well. Small residential lots line the south side of the woods, most of which have been severed from farms. The road along this side of the woods is the main one into the village of Hickory. The trees along the banks of Muskrat Creek upstream of the woods are intact, and the natural course of the stream has not been altered. To the west, farmland is leased out to nearby farmers, and many fields are beginning to grow over in poplar and some pine. A Christmas-tree farm has been started in one corner.

Previous contact with people in the area, and casual encounters with some of the landowners have given an indication that the majority of residents seem to be interested in conservation or at least in the long-term maintenance of the woods and wetland.

The Landowners of Woodpecker Woods and Wetlands

Property #1 (37 hectares/92 acres) is owned by Ron and Hazel Greenbrier, part-time farmers with a young family. Having strong rural roots, they consider themselves conservation minded, but are not ready to do anything just yet about preserving the woodlot on their property. While their definition of conservation may be more management oriented, they are interested in the broad objective of maintaining some land in its natural state. The family is not keen on having a lot of people walking across their farm to gain access to the woods. Their initial response to the landowner-contact representative was cool, as they are suspicious of eco-freaks, government and people from the city.

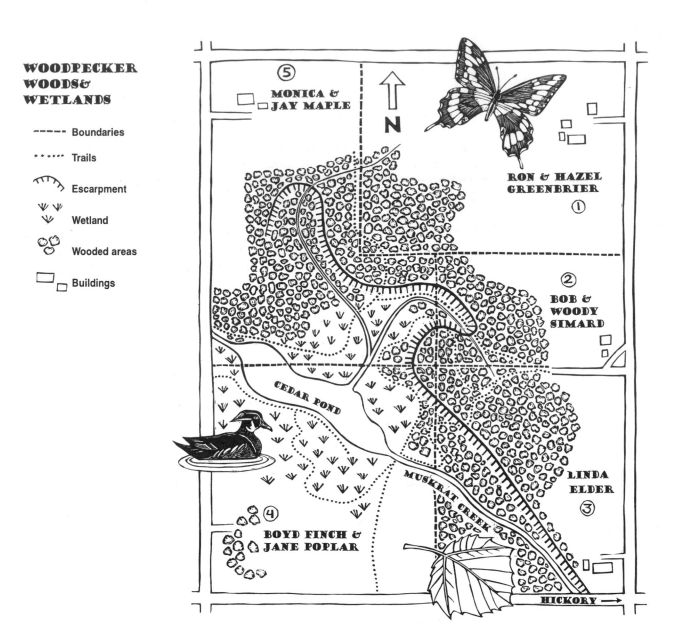

WOODPECKER WOODS & WETLANDS

- – – – – **Boundaries**
- · · · · · **Trails**
- **Escarpment**
- **Wetland**
- **Wooded areas**
- **Buildings**

⑤ MONICA & JAY MAPLE

N

RON & HAZEL GREENBRIER ①

② BOB & WOODY SIMARD

CEDAR POND

MUSKRAT CREEK

LINDA ELDER ③

④ BOYD FINCH & JANE POPLAR

HICKORY →

Property #2 (15 hectares / 37 acres) is owned by Bob and Woody Simard, two brothers in their fifties. They don't know very much about the flora and fauna on their land, but are interested in finding out a bit more. Like the Greenbriers, they are not ready to do anything right away, but will likely sell the place in the future (five to ten years) to move closer to town, perhaps to a retirement community. The Simard property contains a small house and a shed. They have an extensive vegetable garden and a few acres of pasture, which they lease to the Greenbrier family. The road along the south side provides access to the woods at the back of the property, and in the past there was some selective cutting in the woods. The Simards' access road is a private one shared by the Elder property, but it is kept open and is considered the main access to the woods.

Property #3 (33 hectares / 81 acres) is owned by Linda Elder, a local business-woman. She purchased it last year from a family who had lived there for fifty years. There is currently one house on the property, which is hilly and contains the highest point in the woods.

The Ontario Land Tax Reduction Program is designed to help landowners conserve Ontario's special natural heritage.

Tax rebates are offered to landowners who agree to protect the natural heritage values of their property. Eligible lands include provincially significant wetlands, areas designated as Escarpment Natural Areas in the Niagara Escarpment Plan and certain conservation lands owned by non-profit, charitable organizations.

The Management Forest Tax Rebate Program encourages management practices that will protect and enhance the environment on private woodlands. The program offers property tax rebates to owners who manage their forests for long-term environmental benefits.

(See Information Sources.)

Because the ground is very rocky, with several outcrops along the edge of a small escarpment, the land was never farmed, except near the road, where some pasturing took place. Linda is not particularly interested in conservation and purchased the lot as an investment. Her small business in town isn't doing too well, although she always seems to be wheeling and dealing. Active in the community she belongs to the Kiwanis Club and is a member of the local United Way committee. Her long-term plan is to cut most of the timber and subdivide the property into estate lots. The reason she hasn't had some of the trees cut is because the price has been too low, but if things in town slow down, she will find a contractor. The property has good access on three sides and would be easy to subdivide.

Property #4 (30 hectares / 75 acres) is owned by Boyd Finch and Jane Poplar, an elderly couple who live closer to the city. They visit the property often and have had it for a long time. There are no buildings on the lot, although there is a small driveway and clearing where they sometimes park their trailer. They bought the lot for next to nothing from a friend, to use as a summer place for camping and picnicking. Boyd and Jane are interested in conservation. They maintain several trails, have put up wood-duck boxes and are knowledgeable about the flora and fauna of the area. They are members of the local naturalist club.

Jane and Boyd are concerned about preserving the woodland/wetland complex in its entirety. Their land contains the largest portion of wetland, including a part of Muskrat Creek and all of Cedar Pond. In fact, the whole western half of the property is covered by water in early spring and the road is sometimes flooded. The pond and surrounding marsh well known to bird watchers. They are interested in information on the Ontario Conservation Land Tax Reduction Program and the Managed Forest Tax Rebate Program.

Property #5 (34 hectares/85 acres) is owned by Monica and Jay Maple, who have two young children, with a third on the way. The family recently moved to the area to be closer to the city, as both parents work. They are ambivalent about conservation, and protection of the woodlot is not a high priority. They lease three fields to a farmer across the road for pasture. They don't expect to live there for a long time because the house will be too small for their growing family.

Strategies for protecting Woodpecker Woods and Wetlands

The following sections will suggest a variety of techniques, tools and opportunities that could be used to protect Woodpecker Woods and Wetlands. As you will discover, there are a large number of options, each reflecting particular circumstances and financial, social or ecological situations. There are no hard-and-fast rules when pursuing land protection. The only way to begin to understand the complexities is to remain flexible with regard to mixing and matching options, and to realize that each property and landowner is a completely different case. The techniques you use depend largely on the interests of the landowner, as well as on how involved your organization wants to get in the hands-on protection of land. Knowing what your organization wants from the landowner is important (do you want to buy the land, help him/her manage it or just get some assurance of his/her interest in conservation?). The ability of your organization to undertake future management of a property will also play a key role. Many of these issues are raised again in the following pages.

For the sake of simplicity, we will assume first of all that the area has no special designation in the official plan, but the wheels are in motion to have the natural values of Woodpecker Woods and Wetlands recognized in it. However, this may take some time, so a proactive approach through land acquisition and stewardship should be looked at. There are no immediate threats to the woods at the moment, but there is ample evidence of changes to the landscape as a result of the demand for rural-residential housing.

The first step decided upon by your group is to approach Boyd Finch and Jane Poplar, as they have shown interest in protecting the natural areas on their property and they own the most significant portions of the woodland/wetland complex. If they are interested in donating the property, this will boost spirits within your organization, as well as give you some standing in the community. The least-threatened areas are worth pursuing next, and discussions with Linda Elder, owner of the most-threatened property, should also begin, as an agreement with her might take the longest to conclude.

Options for #4, the Finch and Poplar property

Because Jane and Boyd have expressed considerable interest in conservation, do not want to see their property developed in any way and have no apparent heirs, an outright donation is worth investigating. As this is one of the larger parcels in the wetland/woodland complex, it is a good keystone property to secure first.

Objectives:
◆ undertake long-term securement of the property in its natural state;
◆ try to provide a tax break and avoid possible capital-gains liability.

Suggested Technique: Donation
◆ a donation comprises an outright gift of property or part thereof;
◆ to meet Revenue Canada requirements as a charitable donation, the donors cannot retain any monetary interest in the property;
◆ land donors often want and are able to have certain wishes met by recipients of land donations through 'arm's length' agreements;
◆ these special conditions must be considered early on in any land-donation endeavour;
◆ it is always worthwhile to have potential donors set out their wishes in writing prior to any legal work being undertaken;
◆ the value of a donation is determined by an independent appraisal undertaken by a registered appraiser;
◆ diligent work is essential to ensure that a property being donated does not have liabilities that would be assumed on transfer, such as a mortgage, liens or legal action pending;
◆ donor requirements for time frame (i.e., taxation year) and recognition of anonymity should be respected;
◆ always ask landowners to consult with their own financial planner or lawyer regarding what framework is best for them as there are significant income-tax implications related to donations.

Advantages to landowner:
- tax receipt for value of the property, which can be credited toward income taxes over a five-year period;
- permits the owner to reduce estate taxes by removing the value of the land from the estate;
- immense personal satisfaction from the creation of a priceless living legacy for others to enjoy.

Advantages to organization:
- very cost-effective way to acquire title to land.

Disadvantages:
- working with a potential land donor is a long, time-consuming process;
- most donations take several years of developing rapport with landowner;
- must be able to meet conditions;
- negotiating and processing the acceptance of a donation of property is the most complex securement technique;
- negotiating and processing a property donation may require considerable legal help, increasing the cost of the donation.

Options for #1, the Greenbrier property

Since only a portion of this property is of interest for natural-heritage protection, it is unlikely that restriction of activities on the whole property or ownership by your organization are necessary, although having some sort of a buffer zone is a good idea. It is important that current and future activities on the site are compatible with protecting the woods, so a stewardship agreement with an accompanying management plan would be worth pursuing. In the long term, a conservation easement would likely be sufficient to protect the natural values on the property.

An essential part of protecting this property for the future is to remain in touch with the landowner. A stewardship agreement would allow for relatively frequent, focussed contact and would enable your group to be involved in the management decisions affecting the wooded area on the property. There also may be a good chance that a segment of this property could be protected through a part donation or donated severance in the future.

Objectives:
- to educate landowners on the value of the wooded area and raise awareness of the impact of farming practices on the stream and woods;
- to persuade the landowners to maintain woodlot in natural condition (such as leaving dead trees and snags) and to manage it for firewood while protecting the diversity of the forest.

Suggested techniques/tools: Stewardship Agreement and Management Plan

Stewardship Agreement

- a stewardship agreement is designed to maintain the natural area/woodland on the property;
- agreements can be written or verbal and rely on trust between partners;

61

◆ stewardship agreements are generally set up for a specified period of time and may be renewed subject to mutual consent.

Management Plans

◆ management plans can be designed to maintain the natural area/woodland on the property;
◆ this requires working with the owner to develop a management plan for the property that will maintain and enhance the natural features worth protecting while allowing the owners to continue to work their land;
◆ if the property is part of an ANSI, MNR staff are more likely to be willing to give you management advice on the protection of natural-heritage values.

Advantages of both options to landowner:
◆ gain information about property;
◆ can continue to use the property;
◆ not necessarily legally binding and possible to get out of;
◆ often no money involved;
◆ is based on trust and mutual agreement—people dealing with people.

Advantages of both options to organization:
◆ low cost;
◆ does not require legal involvement but is merely a semiformal "understanding" between two or more parties, relying on good-faith practices;
◆ can meet goals and objectives of protection of the property for both landowner and conservation organization;
◆ is a strong first step in long-term protection of the property.

Disadvantages of both options:
◆ not legally binding;
◆ feeling of "goodwill" may not be enough to restrict or limit resource extraction or potentially damaging activities, especially in tough times;
◆ requires regular monitoring and contact with landowner.

Options for #2, the Simard property:

Because this property has good access to the woods and is adjacent to all the others, it would be a good choice for acquisition. This would provide access if severances are undertaken on other properties. Furthermore, it is a relatively small holding, so obtaining fee-simple interest may be financially feasible. On the other hand, the property is under no immediate threat and the landowners are cooperative with the objectives of conservation. Long-term protection might include obtaining a first-right-of-refusal agreement against the eventual purchase, or possibly purchasing the property and then leasing or selling it back with specific conditions on the title.

Objectives:
◆ to educate the landowners about the natural values of the property and make them aware of its importance to the overall integrity of Woodpecker Woods and Wetlands;

◆ to control access to the woods, as well as the adjacent properties;

◆ acquisition through land purchase (fee simple interest) in the long term.

Suggested tools: First-right-of-refusal Agreement, Bargain Sale and Life Estate

First-right-of-refusal (to purchase) Agreement

◆ try to get an agreement where your organization would have the first chance to purchase the land if the owner sells;

◆ the holder of the first-right-of-refusal agreement has a previously agreed upon period of time to enter into an agreement of purchase and sale on the same terms and conditions as the prospective purchaser, or the landowner is free to dispose of the property;

◆ a first-right-of-refusal agreement with a cooperative landowner can usually be secured for a nominal fee;

◆ the ability of a purchaser to move quickly and buy the property (10 to 15 days) is critical in the use of this technique, so a ready source of cash must be available;

◆ the agreement does not have to be registered on title, but it is a good idea to do so if you can afford the legal fees. Having it registered on title allows for possible legal recourse if the terms are not followed;

◆ see sample right-of-refusal agreement next page.

Advantages to landowner:

◆ does not have to be committed to a set purchase price.

Advantage to organization:

◆ is a cost-effective method of "keeping your foot in the door," although the price of the agreement depends on the landowner.

Disadvantages:

◆ short amount of time available to respond when the owner decides to sell;

◆ it is necessary to ensure that any offers by prospective purchasers are bona fide;

◆ there would be an additional cost of legal fees if the agreement is registered on title.

Bargain Sale

◆ a bargain sale is a combined donation and sale;

◆ the value of the property is established through an appraisal, then the property is sold to a charitable organization for less than the appraised value;

◆ this technique is particularly useful for properties where there has been a substantial increase in the value of the property and the owners may be liable for considerable capital gains;

◆ depending on their financial situation, a bargain sale may be able to save them capital-gains taxes as well as provide a tax credit;

◆ critical to this technique is having a solid appraisal that will stand up under close review by Revenue Canada if necessary (see Appraisals page 65);

◆ as this is another form of land purchase (fee-simple interest), please refer to the discussion of advantages and disadvantages on page 67.

Sample of First Right of Refusal

THIS AGREEMENT made the _____day of _____, _____
Between:

_____, hereinafter called "AAA" OF THE FIRST PART

and

_____, hereinafter called "BBB" OF THE SECOND PART

WHEREAS AAA is the owner of the property situated in the Township of_____, in the County of _____

and being comprised of the whole of Lot _____, Concession _____of the said Township and

containing _____acres more or less as described in the Schedule attached hereto ("the Property").

AND WHEREAS BBB has expressed an interest in purchasing the Property from AAA, who has agreed to grant to BBB a right of first refusal in respect thereof subject to the terms and conditions more particularly hereinafter set out.

WITNESSETH that in consideration of the sum of TWO DOLLARS ($2.00) now paid by BBB to AAA, the receipt and sufficiency of which AAA hereby acknowledges, AAA hereby covenants and agrees as follows:
1. If, during the period of six years from the date of this agreement,
(a) AAA receives a bona fide offer or offers to purchase the Property or any part or parts thereof from any party other than his spouse, his children or his children's spouses, which he is prepared to accept; or

(b) AAA makes a bona fide offer or offers to sell the Property or any part or parts thereof or grants a bona fide option or options to purchase the Property or any parts thereof to any party other than his spouse, his children or his children's spouses subject to the right of BBB hereinafter set out which is or are accepted by the offeree or grantee;

he will forthwith advise BBB in writing of all the terms and conditions contained in such offer, offers, option or options, and BBB during the period of fifteen (15) days after the receipt of such written advice shall have the right to be exercised by written notice to AAA to purchase the Property at the price and subject to the terms and conditions contained in such offer, offers, option or options.

2. The agreement of purchase and sale constituted by the exercise of the right of first refusal herein contained shall be subject to compliance with Section 49 of the Planning Act, 1983, as amended time to time.

3. The parties hereto may by mutual consent agree to extend from time to time the period of six years referred to in paragraph one hereof.

4. AAA warrants and represents that no spousal consent is required to this agreement, as the Property is not a matrimonial home within the meaning of Section 18 of the Family Law Act, 1986.

5. Any notice or other communication required or permitted to be given hereunder shall be in writing and shall be given either by delivering the same to the recipient or mailing the same postage prepaid in a government post box to the recipient at the following address:

If to AAA:address

_____

If to BBB:address

_____

6. This agreement shall endure to the benefit of and be binding upon the parties hereto and their respective executors, administrators, successors and assigns.

IN WITNESS WHEREOF the parties hereto have hereunto set their hands and seals.

SIGNED, SEALED AND DELIVERED in the presence of _____

A few tips regarding appraisals:

- use an appraiser from the area;

- use an appraiser who is a current member of the Appraisal Institute of Canada;

- do not pay for the work until you have seen the draft, to ensure that the right property has been appraised (check the property description and sketch with your own information and be certain that the pictures included in the appraisal look like the property you are interested in);

- ask the appraiser if he/she will undertake the work at a discount, as your organization is nonprofit, or ask for a cheque exchange (a method where you pay for the service, but the appraiser donates an equal amount for a tax receipt);

- offer to print the appraiser's logo or wordmark as a thank-you in your next newsletter or announcement of the project.

Advantages to landowner:
- reduction in capital-gains liability, as selling price of property has been reduced;
- tax receipt for donation can be applied against income taxes and spread out over a number of years.

Advantages to organization:
- purchase of property at less than market value.

Disadvantages to landowner:
- less revenue from sale of property as selling price is lower (offset to some extent by the tax receipt).

Appraisals
A real-estate appraisal is an expert's opinion of the fair-market value of a property, based on recent sales of similar properties in the area. The process is basically a comparison, with three or four comparable properties used as benchmarks. The appraiser's opinion on the differences and similarities results in an estimated value for the property of interest. Appraisals are essential for a property purchase but may not always be necessary for donations.

Life Estate
- entails direct purchase of land (acquiring fee-simple interest) with special conditions for past landowners;
- care must be taken to have a legally binding license agreement for the use of the property, which specifies certain terms and conditions and prevents the life interest from being extended to other persons;
- to prevent a severance of the property, the license agreement must be for less than 21 years, but may be renewed;
- a value of the life estate is determined and deducted from the purchase price;
- see examples of conditions that could be included in the license agreement;
- discussion of advantages, disadvantages of a regular land purchase applies to the life-estate tool.

Advantages to landowner:
- retains use of the property for the rest of his/her life.

Advantages to organization:
- vendor may be interested in managing the property for you and acting as steward;
- purchase price is lower than fair-market value, as value of life use of property by vendor is deducted from purchase price.

Disadvantage:
- legal costs can be quite high, as agreement must be detailed.

Options for #3, the Elder Property:

This property is considered to be the most likely to be developed, although the owner has not applied for an amendment to the official plan or a change to the zoning by-law. The owner sees the land as a business investment, and it is unlikely that any persuasion will change her views. Therefore, any tools used to provide for the long-term protection of the property must be financially appealing.

Objectives:

◆ to protect the integrity of the forest as much as possible;

◆ to provide the landowner with a return on investment and not compromise the natural values of the property;

◆ to have the property, which contains almost half of Woodpecker Woods, eventually recognized as environmentally sensitive in the official plan to restrict further development or possible subdivision.

Examples of conditions found in a life-estate agreement

TO HAVE AND TO HOLD the said premises free of any occupation charge in the nature of rent from the date hereof to the date on which the first of the following events occur:

a) the death of the Licensee;

b) the day which is 21 years less one day from the date hereof;

c) the Licensee ceases to use the said premises as his principal residence;

d) the Licensee without the approval of the Licensor ceases to personally occupy the said premises for a period exceeding four weeks in each year; and

e) the substantial damage or destruction of the said premises and the Licensor in its absolute discretion decides that the same shall not be repaired or rebuilt.

THE Licensee covenants with the Licensor to repair and maintain the said premises at his sole cost and expense.
AND to keep up fences.
AND to preform all statute labour.
AND not to cut down timber or trees of any kind whatsoever.
AND to pay for all heat, water, light and other utilities and amenities used in the said premises.
AND that the Licensor may enter and view state of repair.
AND that the Licensee will repair according to notice in writing.
AND will insure and keep insured the said premises against fire, lightning or tempest in an appropriate amount in the joint names of the Licensor and Licensee,

with loss, if any, payable as their respective interests may appear.
AND will not carry on any business on said premises.
AND that he will leave the premises in good repair.
PROVIDED that the Licensee may remove his fixtures, if such removal may be done and is done without injury to the said premises.

AND the Licensee doth hereby further covenant and agree with the Licensor in the manner following, that is to say: THAT the Licensee will during the term of the Licence maintain the land surrounding the buildings in a neat and tidy condition and not allow any waste or refuse to be deposited thereon. AND will during the continuance of said term mow along the fences and in the fence corners on the said lands, keep down all noxious weeds and grasses, which shall grow upon the said premises or on the side of the roads or highways adjacent thereto, and will not sow or permit to be sown any grain infected by smut or containing any foul seeds or noxious weeds, and will not suffer or permit any such foul seeds or noxious weeds to go to seed on the said premises.

AND will carefully protect and preserve all trees on said premises from waste, injury or destruction, and will care for all such trees as often as they require it.

Options: Purchase and Option to Purchase

Purchase of Land (fee-simple interest)

◆ when a nonprofit organization purchases property, there are several things to watch out for. *Creative Conservation: A Handbook for Ontario Land Trusts* provides some good pointers on fee-simple acquisition and some of the issues that need to be dealt with when an organization buys land;

◆ fee-simple interest in land may be limited by certain conditions or by registered interests, such as a mortgage or a long-term lease;

◆ taking title to the property involves responsibilities that may be too onerous for some groups or individuals;

◆ payment of property taxes and management costs may be too great a financial burden for some organizations;

◆ the price of land is influenced by what it can be used for, and it is important to know the designation of the property under the official plan for the municipality or region;

◆ always consider the alternatives to acquisition, especially if funds are not readily available for an outright purchase and ongoing management of the property.

Advantages to landowner:

◆ straightforward real-estate transaction.

Advantages to organization:

◆ purchaser gets full rights to the property and full protection is achieved;

◆ other organizations and government agencies may be able to help out with the management costs, or may be able to take title once the property has been acquired. (The Nature Conservancy of Canada often purchases property, then turns title over to a government agency with specific management conditions attached);

◆ obtaining title of a property will give the organization a standing in the community to lobby for zoning changes;

◆ sometimes a tangible project such as a land purchase provides a focus for fund-raising efforts and helps to rally support from other organizations;

◆ land purchase may be the favoured alternative for many conservation organizations because of its familiarity and the security it provides.

Disadvantages:

◆ the cost of the purchase;

◆ the price of land, especially in some parts of southern Ontario, may be prohibitive to groups or individuals interested in conservation;

◆ not necessarily any tax benefits to landowner who is selling property.

Option to Purchase

- options are legally binding agreements that set a purchase price for a specified time period (see example of wording below);
- the legal agreement prevents the owner from offering the property to another purchaser while fund-raising is taking place;
- the option agreement should include provisions to ensure that the values for which the property is being acquired (e.g., trees) are not destroyed, altered, removed or tampered with prior to the actual purchase (see example wording for provision);
- generally, the landowner is paid a sum of money in return for entering into an option;
- when the option is exercised on or before the specified date by the prospective purchaser, there is an immediate contract of sale on the property, and the parties officially become vendor and purchaser.

Advantages to landowner:
- a legal, signed agreement with a prospective purchaser.

Advantages to organization:
- buys time to undertake fund-raising;
- also buys time to investigate the zoning options.

Disadvantages:
- landowner may want more security than a deposit, or may ask for an unreasonably short period, especially if he/she is anxious to sell the property.

EXAMPLE OF WORDING THAT WOULD BE CONTAINED IN AN OPTION OF PURCHASE AND SALE:

This agreement is subject to a condition in the Purchaser's favour that the Purchaser has obtained funding satisfactory to it within thirty (30) days from the date of acceptance by the Vendor of this agreement. Failing such funding or the waiver of this condition by the Purchaser, this agreement shall be null and void and the deposits shall be paid to the Purchaser and the interest thereon (if any) to the Vendor.

EXAMPLE OF WORDING FOR A PROVISION TO PROTECT NATURAL VALUES ON THE PROPERTY WHILE UNDER AN OPTION TO PURCHASE:

The Vendor covenants and agrees that during the term of this agreement or any extension thereof, the Vendor will do nothing that will or might damage or detract from the natural value or interest of the property. If at any time prior to closing, in the purchaser's opinion, the natural value or interest of the property is destroyed or damaged by any cause whatsoever and to such an extent as to render the land of insufficient interest to the Purchaser, the Purchaser shall have the right to declare this agreement null and void and the deposits with all interest thereon (if any) shall be paid to the Purchaser.

Options for #5, the Maple property

The woodland on this property is not threatened at the moment. A management agreement or plan that includes the current farm activities may be sufficient to protect the property for now. In the long term, a part purchase, a lease, or a purchase with leaseback or sale back would be worth pursuing.

Objectives:

- to educate landowners on the value of the wooded area and raise awareness of the impact of farming practices on the stream and woods;
- to persuade the landowners to maintain the woodlot in a natural condition;
- to restrict development or detrimental activities in the wetland and wooded portions of the property.

Options: Part Purchase, Lease, Purchase (Leaseback or Sale Back, and Conservation Easement)

Part Purchase

- this is a direct purchase under fee-simple-transaction arrangements for a part of the property;
- severancing of the property is usually needed.

Advantage to landowner:

- sells part of the property that perhaps wasn't very useful anyway.

Advantages to organization:

- acquires only the part of the property interested in, not hindered with whole property;
- cheaper than purchasing whole property.

Disadvantages:

- not always easy to get a severance;
- may not be able to include any buffer zones if just the key portions of the property are bought.

Lease

- your organization could rent a piece of property;
- as a tenant, your organization has absolute control over the property during the term of the lease, even priority over the landlord, provided conditions specified in the lease are observed;
- the lease is of a temporary nature, although it may be renewed for successive periods of less than 21 years;
- the conditions of the lease required by the property owner may pose limitations on the use and development of the property;
- leases are used extensively in agriculture and for urban property.

Advantages to landowner:
◆ retains title to the property;
◆ is relatively straightforward to draw up and is a familiar technique.

Advantages to organization:
◆ can be used as a temporary "holding" method while raising funds for more permanent protection;
◆ can be relatively cheap, similar to a management agreement, but with the organization being the tenant.

Disadvantages:
◆ due to the temporary nature of a lease, investments in development and management must be carefully considered in terms of cost-effectiveness over the long term;
◆ could become expensive over the long term if the "rent" is high.

Purchase and Leaseback

◆ involves land purchase and subsequent leasing of all or a portion of the property for a specific purpose (e.g., farming);
◆ very useful technique for dealing with hiking trails or donated trade lands (such lands may be adjacent to a core protected site, such as an existing nature reserve).

Purchase and Sale Back

◆ as with purchase and leaseback above, this requires acquisition of title and the subsequent sale back with restrictive covenants on the title to protect certain features;

◆ a portion of the property may be sold through a severance (this portion may include buildings or features that are not related to the objectives of the project).

Given that these two techniques rely on the same principles, the advantages and disadvantages are discussed together.

Natural Heritage Stewardship Awards have been presented to hundreds of Ontario owners of wetlands, escarpment and other natural areas, in recognition of their exemplary stewardship of these significant areas.

Advantages to landowner:
- ◆ land purchase is relatively straightforward;
- ◆ leasing from the organization that bought the property probably means very little disruption in activity, especially if farming;
- ◆ may not be interested in retaining whole property; for example, landowner may wish to continue living in the farmhouse but not have to worry about the rest of the property.

Advantages to organization:
- ◆ some of the cost of the acquisition can be recouped through the leaseback or sale back;
- ◆ lease or sale may help offset management costs of the rest of the property;
- ◆ can control activities on the property through specific requirements and conditions in the lease agreement or through a restrictive covenant being placed on title.

Disadvantages:
- ◆ requires acquiring title in fee-simple interest.

Conservation Easement

- ◆ an easement is a voluntary agreement between a landowner and a conservation agency to protect the natural values of a property by placing conditions on its management;
- ◆ the method grants only the rights that are specified in the agreement.

Advantages to landowner:
- ◆ retains title to the property;
- ◆ may be able to receive an income-tax receipt from a nonprofit organization.

Advantages to organization:
- ◆ may be less costly than acquiring title and only deals with those issues that are of interest;
- ◆ can be obtained in perpetuity;
- ◆ can be purchased or donated.

Disadvantages:
- ◆ may be costly if the rights being acquired are considered of high value;
- ◆ have not yet been used for conservation purposes.

This chapter ends with another success story—about Sue Bryan and the Thunder Bay Field Naturalists, who were able to protect a significant property in the north of Ontario.

Sue Bryan

Preserving the home of Maymaygwayshi

aymaygwayshi is known as the mischievous spirit. According to the Ojibwa, he lives at the mouth of the Nipigon River in a secret tunnel. Legend has it that Maymaygwayshi is responsible for introducing lake trout into Lake Nipigon, by stealing fish out of the nets of the Anishnabeg (known today as the Ojibwa) and taking them through his secret tunnel from Lake Superior to Lake Nipigon.

The legend appears to have some basis in fact. A scuba diver from Schreiber, Ryan LeBlanc, discovered that there is indeed a cave 20 feet under the water, on a cliff face at the mouth of the Nipigon River. At the edge of the cave LeBlanc found skeletons of fish, possibly left by Maymaygwayshi.

Maymaygwayshi would no doubt be pleased with the actions of Sue Bryan of the Thunder Bay Field Naturalists. By day, Sue is a doctor with a specialty in anaesthesiology. But in her spare time, she enjoys the great outdoors—plants, birds, canoeing, hiking, the opposite of what she calls her "indoor, high-tech" day job.

Sue Bryan and the field naturalists have purchased 320 acres of land at the mouth of the Nipigon River, where the underwater cave and a pictograph of Maymaygwayshi are found. The naturalists unofficially call the site the "Nipigon River-mouth Nature Reserve." They bought it for $47,452 with financial assistance from the Natural Heritage Challenge Fund of the Ontario Heritage Foundation. The fund provided four dollars for every one dollar raised by the naturalist club. In addition, the field naturalists had to pay all other costs associated with the land purchase, such as legal fees, the appraisal and so on.

The club also had to provide a scientific justification for preserving the site by writing up a natural area inventory. Along with rare plants, birds and ferns, the site contains a famous set of pictographs—over 40 altogether, including the one of Maymaygwayshi.

Bryan says the inventory was "the fun side" of the work —"learning how to put together bird, plant and mammal inventories. I got into all sorts of neat activities, such as plant collecting and using live traps to identify mammals, then let them go again."

The red tape involved in purchasing the site was not fun. In fact, it dragged on over 15 months. There were two parcels of land, with two sets of owners. The site was first "discovered" by another club member, who saw one of the properties advertised for sale in the newspaper. In October 1992, she took Sue out in a canoe to look at it, since it's not accessible by road.

The excitement Sue felt on that trip comes through even today in her voice. "Lo and behold, it was a place I already knew. I hadn't realized it was for sale or that it was privately owned. It's considered to be the second-most-important pictograph site on the north shore of Lake Superior. The other one is at Agawa and it's already protected (in a provincial park). While we were there we happened to notice an osprey fishing and a bald eagle flying around."

Along with rare plants, birds and ferns, the site contains a famous set of pictographs —over 40 altogether—including one of Maymaygwayshi.

The field naturalists decided the adjoining piece of property should also be purchased, because the pictographs were near the property line.

Sue tells of her first attempt to write to the two property owners, suggesting that they donate the land in exchange for a tax receipt. "Well, you can imagine how far that got. They didn't even answer the letter." So she proceeded to negotiate a sale price, then put in an offer to purchase conditional on receiving financial support from the Ontario Heritage Foundation. Then she waited.

As the deadline on the offer was about to run out, Sue had to enlist police help. Two older men from Baltimore, Maryland, owned one of the lots, and one of them had died since the club's offer was put in. The partner still living wasn't answering the club's urgent letters suggesting he get on with signing the deal. So, Sue says, she "phoned the local police to ask if they could help in finding this missing person. They got the Baltimore police out and hunted him down at some relative's house, and the guy called up and the deal was in, just in time."

As well as purchasing the property, the Thunder Bay naturalists have convinced the MNR to shelve a plan to build a logging road through the site. The surrounding area now won't be logged, and without a road, the site will remain accessible only by water. They're also talking to the MNR about using the ministry's parks program to preserve even more of the natural area—for Maymaygwayshi, and for future generations of naturalists like Sue Bryan.

Information sources

Guide to the Ontario Conservation Land Tax Reduction Program, 1995 and Guidelines for the 1996 Managed Forest Tax Rebate Program
Contact the Subsidies Management Branch, MMAH,
1-800-268-8959 or (416) 971-8071.

Subsidies Management Branch, MMAH
777 Bay Street, 12th Floor
Toronto, Ontario, M5G 2E5

Centre for Land and Water Stewardship
University of Guelph
Guelph, Ontario, N1G 2W1
(519) 824-4120 ext. 2702
Director/Chair: Dr. Stewart Hilts

Couchiching Conservancy,
333 Mary Street, Orillia,
Ontario L3V 3E9

Useful documents

Attridge, Ian. 1995 *Guide to Using Conservation Covenants and Easements in Ontario.* Centre for Land and Water Stewardship (in draft)

Attridge, Ian C. and Thea M. Silver, Maria MacRae and Kenneth W. Cox. 1995. *Canadian Legislation for Conservation Covenants, Easements and Servitudes. The Current Situation.* North American Wetlands Conservation Council. Ottawa

Barret, Thomas S. and Janet Diehl. *The Conservation Easement Handbook.* 1988. Trust for Public Land. San Francisco

Canadian Wildlife Service. 1995. *Donation of Ecologically Sensitive Land in Canada; Procedures for Implementing New Provisions of the Income Tax Act of Canada.* Environment Canada. Ottawa

Hilts, S., T. Moull T. J. Rzadki and M. Van Patter. 1991. *Natural Heritage Landowner Contact Training Manual.* Natural Heritage League. Toronto

Reid, Ron and Stewart Hilts. 1990. *Land Stewardship Options.* Greater Toronto Area Greenlands Strategy. Toronto.

Reid, Ron. 1987. *Conservation Easements: A Report on the Conservation Easements Implementation Project.* Ontario Heritage Foundation. Toronto

Reid, Ron and Brad Peterson. 1994. *Natural Heritage Action Plan.* Couchiching Conservancy. Orillia

Swaigen, John. 1979. *Preserving Natural Areas in Ontario: Private Ownership and Public Rights.* Canadian Environmental Law Research Foundation. Toronto.

The Trust for Public Land. 1995. *Doing Deals: A Guide to Buying Land for Conservation.* Land Trust Alliance. Washington D.C.

Tingley, D., F.P. Kirby and R. Hupfer. 1986. *Conservation Kit: A Legal Guide to Private Conservancy.* Alberta Environmental Law Centre. Edmonton, Alberta. (Environmental Law Centre, #202, 10110-124 Street, Edmonton, Alberta, T5N 1P6)

CONCLUSION

Education & Awareness

he final message of this guide is about the roles that education and awareness play in the protection of wetlands and woodlands. The value of educating people about the significance of natural habitat cannot be underestimated. The FON has run a focussed campaign for the protection of wetlands for at least 15 years. During that time we have seen attitudes change about the need to protect wetlands, as people became more conscious of their value. The conviction held by many diverse groups that wetlands should be protected was finally acknowledged in 1992, when the Wetlands Policy Statement was released. We must continue to raise awareness of the issues around habitat conservation. Woodlands in southern Ontario have not been given the same amount of attention or afforded equivalent protection as wetlands. It is crucial that the value of both be widely understood.

Education and awareness can often be achieved through simple measures — club meetings with guest speakers, slide shows at schools, general displays, educational camps, as well as nature walks and field trips that encourage individuals to appreciate the unique qualities of wetland and woodland ecosystems.

Conservation organizations playing a leading role in education could:

◆ publish information booklets;

◆ produce posters and brochures;

◆ establish nature interpretation and educational centres;

◆ conduct clinics and workshops to educate the public, local officials and developers;

◆ respond to issues raised in the newspapers by writing letters to the editor;

◆ sponsor public forums where environmental issues are discussed;

◆ participate in landowner contact programs;

◆ publish a newsletter that covers articles on recent research or policy issues.

By providing such information, your group can generate publicity and show its strength. All of these activities serve to educate group members, as well as the public.

KEITH DISCIPLINE

Volunteers building plant enclosures to keep out carp and sediment in Second Marsh.

Another activity that stimulates environmental awareness and is often undertaken by local naturalists clubs is habitat enhancement. Whole families can participate and can see the benefits of their work. Such projects include stream clearing, bank stabilization, fencing and signing significant natural areas, garbage clean-up, erecting nesting boxes, and planting trees, shrubs and wildflowers. Organizations seeking more extensive projects can participate in native-species revegetation, seed propagation and rehabilitation of natural communities for increasing and maintaining wildlife and fish species. Demonstration projects can be used to teach the techniques to other landowners who are considering wetland and woodland restoration. Most importantly, these projects demonstrate practices that can be replicated in other situations.

For our last profile we would like to introduce two individuals who have been educating people about the natural world for a long time, Jean and Nelson Maher.

PROFILE

Jean and Nelson Maher

Knowing and understanding the natural world has been a passion for Jean and Nelson (Nels) Maher since childhood, and they believe that passing on such knowledge is a cornerstone of protection. As Nels puts it, "If you educate people (about the natural world) and they take an interest, then they will fight for it."

For more than 40 years, the Mahers have been introducing people to both the wonders of nature and to specific "hot spots" in Grey and Bruce counties. Nels, for example, has been involved in Scouting for all those decades and notes that, for him, the program has always been about exploring the out-of-doors. At the same time, the Mahers have led numerous outings in the area for the FON, introducing people to the bogs and fens of the Bruce Peninsula as well as to Nels's passion, ferns. "Ferns are an indicator plant," he explains. "If you see certain ones, you know you're standing at a hot spot"— an area with large quantities of ferns or one rich in diversity.

You can only value what you know, the Mahers say. "People who never get out of their cars and walk a swamp or woodlot will never know what's missing" in the natural landscape. And because they have made the effort to know the area around their home in Owen Sound, the Mahers are also quick to notice — and act on — detrimental changes. "I took the city to task for allowing home building in an area where the backyards would project into the Niagara Escarpment buffer," Nels notes.

It's not uncommon in Owen Sound for homes to back on to the escarpment, Jean points out, and "a lot of people value having a bit of nature behind them" and will leave natural areas untouched. It's an observation the Mahers have applied in their dealings with other landowners. Nels can recall a number of cases where he and Jean have made such individuals aware and appreciative of the natural-heritage value of their land. Asking for permission to bring small groups in to see orchids or ferns can also "make them feel kind of special," and heighten their interest in preserving the natural values of their property.

Private stewardship, in fact, is another issue in which the Mahers are well versed. They have assisted Jean's brother for years in his efforts to create habitat on the family farm to the south of Owen Sound. Nels shows with pride the fine fern garden growing behind the farmhouse (some were already there; the others were grown from spores), as well as a string of naturalized ponds and a pine plantation modified by cutting gaps and planting acorns that have developed over two decades into healthy young oaks. "It's nice to be able to keep checking a grove of trees that you planted," Nels says. "It lets you see the value of your work. And it can also show you where you have made mistakes."

It's that kind of long-term view that the Mahers find sadly lacking in a lot of current resource management. Contractors working in local woodlots, they say, are motivated to get the maximum amount of wood out in the shortest period, causing lasting damage to the woodlot. The Mahers know from personal observations on Jean's family's farm that there is a better way, and they are always keen to share that knowledge.

"People who never get out of their cars and walk a swamp or woodlot will never know what's missing"

Looking back, Nels says he is deeply indebted to those who spurred his interest in nature, from naturalist "elders" to the father of childhood native friends from Cape Croker who showed him varieties and uses of plants. The Mahers continue to pass on that knowledge through their involvement with Scouts and field naturalists, and through projects such as naturalizing city parks, building boardwalks, as well as creating and maintaining nature trails. Nels and Jean are promoting environmental awareness all the time, whether it be through their nature talks and slide presentations or by leading nature hikes and distributing fern posters and checklists. Enhancing people's knowledge of the natural world is part of their day-to-day life.

Information sources

CBC Educational Sales
Box 500, Station A, Toronto, Ontario, M5W 1E6
(416) 205-6384 phone, (416) 205-3482 fax

Centre for Environmental Education
Department of Elementary and Secondary Education
Murray State University, Murray, KY, 42071, USA
(502) 762-2747 phone, (502) 762-3889 fax

Chickadee and *Owl*
56 The Esplanade, Suite 304, Toronto, Ontario, M5E 1A7

Environment Canada, Inquiry Centre
10 Wellington Street, 1st Floor, Ottawa, Ontario, K1A 0H3
(819) 953-9995 phone, (819) 953-2225 fax

Federation of Ontario Naturalists
355 Lesmill Road, Don Mills, Ontario, M3B 2W8
(416) 444-8419 phone, (416) 444-9866 fax

Green Teacher
95 Robert Street, Toronto, Ontario, M5S 2K5
(416) 960-1244 phone, (416) 925-3474 fax

Ontario Agri-Food Education
P.O. Box 460, 144 Townline Road, Milton, Ontario, L9T 4Z1
(905) 878-1510 phone, (905) 878-0342 fax

Ontario Ministry of the Environment and Energy
Public Information Centre, 135 St. Clair Avenue West,
1st Floor, Toronto, Ontario, M4V 1P5
416) 323-4321 phone, (416) 323-4564 fax

Nirv Centre
401 Richmond Street West, Suite 104,
Toronto, Ontario M5V 3A8,
(416) 596-0212 phone, (416) 596-1374 fax

Useful documents

Federation of Ontario Naturalists. 1994. *Why Wetlands? Education Kit.* Federation of Ontario Naturalists. Don Mills

Federation of Ontario Naturalists. 1995. *Soil Conservation Education Kit.* Federation of Ontario Naturalists. Don Mills

Federation of Ontario Naturalists. 1992. *Carolinian Canada Teacher's Guide.* Federation of Ontario Naturalists. Don Mills

Federation of Ontario Naturalists. 1992. Hands on Nature Series (*Introducing Birds, Introducing Insects, Introducing Trees, Introducing Flowers* and *Introducing Reptiles*). Federation of Ontario Naturalists. Don Mills

Pembina Institute for Appropriate Development. 1995. *The Canadian Environmental Education Catalogue.* Pembina Institute for Appropriate Development. Drayton Valley, Alberta

Appendices

Game of Letters

Writing a News Release

List of Acronyms

Writing letters to government ministers need not be drudgery. Here's how to create dynamic letters that get results

Game of Letters

BY RON REID

So you're upset with the government's record on protecting wilderness areas. Maybe they've just caved in again to yet another corporate polluter. Or they are threatening to cancel a valuable program. You want to do something to help change their ways, but the enormity of the task makes success look hopeless. What can you do?

One of the most effective weapons, readily available and proven by the test of time, is simply a letter to the various ministers responsible for protecting the environment. Such letter writing can become a fine art, but most of us are a little uncertain just how to begin.

Do letters really count for anything? You bet they do! A senior Ontario cabinet minister once told a group of us, "I look to letters to tell me how much people care about an issue." The implication is clear—if ministers receive dozens of letters on one side of a subject, they have a measure of their constituents' feelings and a basis for action.

But why write a minister, when he or she probably doesn't know anything about your particular gripe anyway? Well, for several reasons, depending on the circumstances. You may be unsure just who within the bureaucracy deals with your problem, and writing to the minister is the best way to get it channelled properly the first time round. You might want to shake up some civil servants who have been unsympathetic or downright unhelpful in earlier dealings. Even though these same people may write the response for the minister, his or her involvement can have a wondrous effect in changing their viewpoint. Often you may want to write a politician as part of an organized campaign, to demonstrate the strength of numbers holding your view. And finally, you can write as a stimulating way to exercise your creative flair, often with environmentally beneficial results as a bonus.

But what if you're uncertain of all the technical complexities surrounding an issue? Not to worry. You probably know as much about it as the minister, and anyway civil servants are supposed to be paid to help you understand the technical details. One of the biggest hurdles to effective letter writing is the groundless fear that you have to be an expert to discuss an issue, a fear all too often cultivated by civil servants.

Cast out such thoughts! We live in a democracy where everyone has the right to set goals and to urge action toward these goals. The experts should be telling us how to get where we want to go, but they have no special claim on naming the destination. If you feel strongly that wildlife should be preserved, or the waters of Lake Ontario made clean again, or whatever, feel free to speak up. The most important role of politicians is to set these goals, and decide their priority, and then to instruct, cajole, harangue, and bully the bureaucracy into accomplishing them. To do that they need your help, often for direction and moral support, but seldom for technical expertise.

What then should your letters contain? The contents vary according to their purpose, but in general they should be relatively short, forceful and to the point. Be as specific as possible without being tedious, and if you have the talent to be witty, a little humour never hurts.

If you can praise the minister's record, even by suggesting that this particular action is out of character, do so. If you can link the subject of your letter to other government actions, policy stances or statements by other ministers, be sure to suggest these links. Local examples are especially effective, because they convey the usefulness of your suggestions. ("If we'd only had this legislation when poor old Uncle Walt's well got poisoned back in '88...")

If you're uncertain of your technical basis, ask leading questions instead of making statements. In any case, be sure to put in questions so that the minister has to respond.

One of the biggest hurdles to effective letter writing is the groundless fear that you have to be an expert to discuss an issue, a fear all too often cultivated by civil servants.

ost important, be specific about what you want him or her to do. The most common weakness of letters to politicians is their failure to identify a specific request, to which the minister must react. Even if you are unsure of exactly what action is needed to correct your concern, try to force a specific response. (For example, you could ask what options the ministry has examined to deal with this problem, and the advantages and disadvantages that they see in each option.)

How spiteful and vindictive should you be? On the first letter, especially if you are opening a new subject, I'd suggest that you give the minister the benefit of the doubt. Be forceful but positive ("I'm sure you agree that this kind of protective measure will benefit us all...").

If your first response is particularly asinine, or if some minister has a consistently bad record, a colourful hatchet job may be the only recourse. Creatively pouring all your venom into a political letter can be therapeutic, even though it's seldom especially effective. And you have to be prepared for the occasional backlash—one particularly vicious letter writer got a fast response from the minister inviting her to telephone and say those things in person!

What can you expect in response to a first letter? Undoubtedly, a long wait. Ministers are notoriously slow in answering mail. At the federal level, they now even acknowledge the receipt of your letter by an assistant so that you don't give up hope as the weeks roll by. If you hit a sore spot in the government's thick hide, expect either an unusually long wait, while they sort it all out, or a surprisingly short one, to try to fob you off quickly.

Ministers' responses are usually of three varieties—affirmative, agreeing with your stance (seldom); zero, ignoring all your questions and saying absolutely nothing (tried fairly frequently); and bafflegab, when they swamp you with technical details and excuses (would probably be tried more often but too much work). The overwhelming odds are that your first response just won't be satisfactory.

Ministers live in the fond hope that you'll just go away. But don't give up, the fun is just beginning. Go back to your original letter, and pull out all the questions the minister didn't answer. Point out inconsistencies between his or her response and others you have received on the subject. If you're lucky, there will be inconsistencies in the minister's letter itself—point those out too. Refute his or her arguments—there are always weak spots—and re-emphasize the desirability of your goals.

If you're concerned about winning an issue, it's the second letter, and the third, that count, because they make the minister and his or her advisers really look at what you're saying, rather than just fobbing you off. These subsequent letters give your creative genius a chance to really shine, responding to some of the incredibly silly things that politicians are wont to say when they're not paying close attention. Letter writing is like a slow game of Ping-Pong—always try to keep lobbing it back to your opponents in their weakest spot.

One easy way to increase the effectiveness of all your letters is to copy them to other interested parties. After all, you don't want to waste all that creative genius on only one minister. Send copies to the leaders or critics of both opposition parties—it keeps them informed, and sometimes they go after the minister for you in the legislature. If you are dealing with a split jurisdiction or you are quoting another minister, send him or her a copy as well—nobody likes to be embarrassed in front of colleagues. If you are having trouble with a particular minister, keep him or her alert by sending a copy to the premier. If you're dealing with an issue of local interest, your newspaper editor will usually willingly print a copy of the letter. And if you're dealing with an issue of interest to a conservation group, send a copy to their staff as well. It keeps their spirits up, and you might even get some free help.

If you are deadly serious about accomplishing results with your letters, the three R's apply: be right, reasonable and repetitive. But don't forget to have fun along the way.

Some budding authors sponsor letter-writing parties, to stimulate creative sparks and see who can come up with the wittiest letter. Others prefer the Lone Ranger approach, rising restlessly in the middle of the night to dash off a letter by E-mail, or holing up in a favourite armchair with a laptop or a writing pad.

Whatever the technique, an enthusiastic approach to letter writing can create a new art form, and increase the effectiveness of us all in championing conservation causes. The pen is still mightier than the sword, and its cut and thrust can be almost as painful if aimed in the right direction. So dust off your favourite cause, pull up a chair, and make that paper or keyboard sing—there are politicians by the dozens just waiting to hear from you!

Letter writing is like a slow game of Ping-Pong— always try to keep lobbing it back to your opponents in their weakest spot.

reprinted from *Seasons*, Winter 1995

Writing a News Release

Who, What, When, Where and Why

Important Information in Descending Order

Miscellaneous Information

1) The title, date of release, name and phone number of contact person (both work and home) should be listed.

2) The first paragraph must contain the 5 "Ws" in it: Who, What, When, Where, and Why.

3) Information should be given in descending order of interest.

4) Be exact. State accurately the date of the event, ensure all names are given in full, correctly spelled and with their titles.

5) Be objective, not subjective.

6) Type your news release on one side of the page only, with at least one inch margins.

7) Your news release should not be longer than two typed pages.

8) Distribute the news release widely: large and small newspapers, local radio and television.

Advantages

- free publicity
- wide circulation
- news coverage lends clout

Disadvantages

- not appropriate for small audiences
- may not be the best method to reach your target audience

List of Acronyms

Areas of Natural and Scientific Interest (ANSIs)

Canadian Wildlife Service (CWS)

Coalition on the Niagara Escarpment (CONE)

Conservation Authority (CA)

Environmental and Ecological Advisory Committee (EEAC)

Environmental Youth Corps (EYC)

Environmentally Sensitive Areas (ESAs)

Federation of Ontario Naturalists (FON)

Long Point Bird Observatory (LPBO)

Ministry of the Environment and Energy (MOEE)

Ministry of Municipal Affairs and Housing (MMAH)

Ministry of Natural Resources (MNR)

Natural Heritage Information Centre (NHIC)

Natural Resources Information Centre (NRIC)

Niagara Escarpment Commission (NEC)

Niagara Escarpment Plan (NEP)

Ontario Municipal Board (OMB)